WITHDRAWN

Communicational Analysis and Methodology For Historians

by L. G. HELLER

New York: New York University Press
1972

P
41
.H38

TO
PROFESSOR HOWARD ADELSON

FOREWORD

This book had its origin in a request by Professor Howard Adelson, Chairman of the Department of History of the City College of the City University of New York, that I deliver a lecture to some graduate students on the applications of linguistic techniques to the reconstruction and analysis of history and prehistory. With this end in view, I started jotting down a few formulas and examples, intending to mimeograph some brief notes for the convenience of the class. From time to time, as thoughts relevant to the topic occurred, additional observations went into the folder. By the time the date assigned to the lecture had arrived, the more than two hundred pages reposing in the file suggested that something more than a mimeographed guide might be necessary. The gratifying enthusiasm of the students and the friendly encouragement of Professor Adelson and also of the latter's brother, Professor Judah Adelson, of the State University of New York at New Paltz, induced me to expand and polish the "notes" in the hope that possibly other historians, as well perhaps as other social scientists, might find them useful and interesting.

This treatise makes no pretense of either completeness or great profundity. On the contrary, I have attempted to simplify—possibly even to oversimplify—in the interest of clarity. Occasionally, unfortunately, I have lapsed into the technical jargon of professional linguists, despite my awareness that such jargon may occasion some discomfort to potential readers. The only justification for this departure from the clarity criterion is an intense preoccupation with precision and accuracy. Like the proverbial iceberg which reportedly lies mainly beneath the surface, not visible to the observer, the technical jargon holds a wealth of conceptual precision, most of it not immediately apparent to the uninformed reader. Although one could readily paraphrase in one manner or another some of the terms, the circumlocution would necessarily either be so lengthy as to be cumbersome or would leave out much that linguists regard as critical. The occasional digressive explanations and definitions may suffice for those historians who do not have training in linguistic theory. A more thoroughgoing and direct presentation of such information would have exceeded the intent and scope of this volume.

A few additional comments may be appropriate here regarding the arrangement and content of the material in this book. After the introductory "General Observations" (Section 1), five sections focus on "Reconstruction," arbitrarily divided into "Chronological" (Section 2), "Geographical" (Section 3), "Sociocultural," i.e., the reconstruction of the relevant features of the entire system (Section 5), "Monanthropical," i.e., the reconstructive identification of the individual and his place within his own society (Section 6), and "Graphological," i.e., the decipherment of unknown writing systems (Section 7). One part—"Communicational Systems in Perspective" (Section 4)—could well have preceded the reconstructive parts. However, it seemed strategically undesirable to force the nonlinguist to wade through too much linguistic technology before showing him that the effort was worth his while. The theoretical considerations of Section 4 were necessary, though, for an understanding of other material, hence the interpolation at precisely the point in which the section appears.

Section 8, "Linguistic–Nonlinguistic Relationships," may provide some perspective as to the profound and long-lasting repercussions in language of any change. There it will be seen how an event as remote in time as the Black Plague of the fourteenth century is still causing chain reaction in current English, forcing a restructuring of the pronominal and verbal as well as other systems to this very day.

Section 9, "Linguistic Systems as Analytic Models," presents a somewhat speculative line of potential research that seeks an understanding not about this or that particular sociocultural system but rather about the structures and dynamics of sociocultural systems generally, which seem to obey certain in-built structure-dictated laws so regularly that some note seemed called for, especially since this regularity poses problems of predictability. Because the field of systems analysis of this kind has developed so recently, only two simple examples appear in this book, more for the sake of alerting the reader to certain contemporary lines of thought than of providing him with currently useful tools. The theory inherent in the analogue of Verner's Law should by no means be underestimated, however; it has already served as the basis for some accurate predictions which I have made jointly with Professor James Macris of Clark University and the College of the Holy Cross. Nevertheless, this kind of book did not appear appropriate for extended presentation of what must at best be controversial. Therefore the section is deliberately kept short.

The last section, "Language Classification," considers the different theoretical bases for grouping languages, and provides charts of the interrelationships of at least some of the larger families of genetically related systems. Scholars have identified well over four thousand different languages, each worthy of full treatment. Needless to say, only the most cursory outline can appear here.

For reasons which will become obvious, this book deliberately restricts its aims chiefly to methodological concerns or to matter that is necessary as background for that end. The fullest possible treatment of each of the topics would constitute nothing less than the entire history and prehistory of mankind.

I wish to express my thanks to both Professor Howard Adelson, to whom the volume is dedicated, and Professor Judah Adelson; their lengthy discussions, sharp insights, and constant interest have contributed much to whatever merits this book may possess. A debt of gratitude is likewise due to Mr. Norman Young, a modern Maecenas, who encouraged me to keep plugging away at the writing of this and other books, and who has provided secretarial service and other invaluable assistance through his business office. Thanks are also due to Mrs. Agnes Stangarone, whose ability to decipher my handwriting and to translate it into intelligible typescript deserves mention in the same section (7) as that devoted to the greatest decipherments of all time.

CONTENTS

1. GENERAL OBSERVATIONS   1

2. CHRONOLOGICAL RECONSTRUCTION   6
   2.1. Agenetic Considerations   7
      2.11. Simple Dating Procedures   7
      2.12. Reconstruction of the History of Fields
         or Influences   9
   2.2. Agenetic Versus Genetic Considerations   12
   2.3. Genetic Dating   15
      2.31. Sequential Splitting and Comparative
         Methodology   16
      2.32. Sequential Differentiation and Internal
         Reconstruction   19
      2.33. Percentile Retention Averaging:
         Glottochronology   22

3. GEOGRAPHICAL RECONSTRUCTION   31
   3.1. Genetic Relationships   32
   3.2. The Primal Homeland   33
   3.3. The Path of Migration   36
   3.4. Ancient Contacts   39
   3.5. The Provenience and Travels of the Individual   41
   3.6. Geoethnography   46
      3.61. Toponymics: The Study of Place Names   47
      3.62. Topidionymics: The Study of the
         Distribution of Personal Names   49
   3.7. Physical Topography   51

4. COMMUNICATIONAL SYSTEMS IN PERSPECTIVE   57
   4.1. Manifesting Systems   58
      4.11. Non-concept-correlated Building Blocks   60

4.12. Concept-correlated Building Blocks   69
4.2. Cognitive Systems   72

5. SOCIOCULTURAL RECONSTRUCTION   76
5.1. Monochronic, Monosystemic Analysis   78
5.2. Monochronic, Di- or Polysystemic Analysis   84
5.3. Polychronic, Diasystemic Analysis   86
5.4. Diachronic Projection from Synchronic,
      Polysystemic Analysis   87

6. MONANTHROPICAL RECONSTRUCTION   92

7. GRAPHOLOGICAL RECONSTRUCTION   102
7.1. A Glossographic Typology   103
      7.11. The Language   103
      7.12. The Writing System   106
7.2. General Observations Regarding Decipherment 112

8. LINGUISTIC–NONLINGUISTIC RELATIONSHIPS:
    The Long-range Impact of Nonlinguistic Events on
    Language   122

9. LINGUISTIC SYSTEMS AS ANALYTIC MODELS   130
9.1. The Rank-size Law   131
9.2. A Sociocultural Analogue of Verner's Law   132

10. LANGUAGE CLASSIFICATION   137
10.1. The Basis of Classification   137
       10.11. Geographical Distribution   137
       10.12. Genetic Relationship   137
       10.13. Typological Structure   140
10.2. A Survey of Some Major Classifications   143

1. GENERAL OBSERVATIONS

Language eventually encodes and encapsulates most—perhaps all—of the relevant features of the sociocultural system of its speakers. Furthermore, even when the system changes, as it inevitably does, and the language restructures to reflect that change, the language itself nevertheless retains certain residues that preserve the history of both language and culture. This history is there for the analyst who knows the code to read and decipher—preserved for as long as any remnant of the language still exists.

Every time anyone speaks or writes, he exhibits *(a)* evidence of the history of the entire culture to which he belongs and *(b)* a total reflection of his own place within his own times. The extent to which this double statement holds true is rarely appreciated by the nonlinguist (and here the term *linguist* is being used to denote the professional analyst of language, not the polyglot—one who writes or speaks two or more languages). For example, I frequently open certain linguistic courses by writing on the blackboard a sentence or even a fragment of a sentence from some writer, past or present. I then invite my students to describe the writer, the culture of his times, the migrations of his ancestors, the homeland of these ancestors, their cultural contacts, and so on. I may even ask the students if the writer himself was short or tall, if he lived on the second floor or the third, and so forth. Part of the presentation, of course, represents mere showmanship designed to capture the interest of the students, but the techniques used and the principles on which they rest represent sound scholarship and the basic insights of a newly developing science. Let us take a typical example.

"Whan that Aprille with his shoures soote . . ."
Here one has only the first line, not even a full sentence, of Geoffrey Chaucer's "Prologue" to *The Canterbury Tales,* written around the

year 1387. The *Tales* themselves are well known to generations of suffering students in English or American schools, since they serve as the introduction to many elementary English literature survey courses. What information then can be abstracted from these few words?

The most obvious fact is that this is late-fourteenth-century English, but from only three words of this line, one can identify through a delimitational technique—a type of linguistic triangulation—the home of the author. The first two letters of *whan, wh,* indicate that Chaucer probably did not come from the Northern area (see Fig. 1) where *qu* was more regular. The *a* specifies that he was not from the West Midland territory. The *sh* of *shoures* proves that he was neither from a Northern area—a confirmation of the first observation—nor from Northeast Midland (otherwise *s* would have been used). The *s* of *soote* proves that the author was not a native of the Southern or Kentish territories nor from a limited portion of Southwest Midland (otherwise he would have used *z*). Thus by simple elimination, only the Southeast Midland area is left. We know from nonlinguistic sources, of course, that this was Chaucer's home, but had other sources been lacking, we could have unhesitatingly provided the same information just by a glance at the three words of the first line, as indicated. If we were to look at additional lines we could see that he spent much time in Kent, although he was not originally from that area. Nevertheless, for illustration purposes let us stay with just the one line.

The word *whan* also shows that the language belongs to the Indo-European family, which includes Italic, Greek, Indo-Iranian, Balto-Slavic, Anatolian, Celtic, and other groups, since the $*k^wom$, to which *whan* (a variant of the form underlying the Modern English *when*) traces back, had cognates in the other branches, e.g., Proto-Indo-European $*k^wom$ > Early Latin *quom,* Classical Latin *cum,* 'when'). This linguistic family laid great stress on time measurement —a feature not found in all linguistic groups as indicated not only by their language but even by their culinary—that's right, culinary —and other cultural traits. For example, in some cultures that omit temporal observation from the closed systems and obligatory portions of their language ("closed systems" and "obligatory parameters" will be explained later), people may invite one to lunch, but they

Fig. 1   MIDDLE ENGLISH DIALECTS
(After Moore and Marckwardt, p. 112.)

do not say—nor would they even consider saying—that the meal will begin precisely at noon or at 12:30 or at any other specific time. Their guests may wander in at almost any time—ten o'clock (by our reckoning, not theirs) eleven, two, three, four, or whenever. The hostess, however, does not become frantic because the steak may burn: she simply keeps a stew simmering all day long, and when (note how often we use the word *when*) her guests arrive, the food is there.

The word *that*, likewise, represents an Indo-European feature, one deriving from *to-to-*, a reduplicated form of the original simple demonstrative *to. This reduplication took place repeatedly in every subbranch of Indo-European and probably reflected a desire to reinforce the foregrounding impact. The *tud* (earlier *tod) of Latin *istud* 'that' derives from this *to-to, but was further reinforced by the *is*, itself a complex form meaning 'that.' In other words the single word *istud* of Latin represents the resultant of successive reinforcements equivalent to 'that, that, that, that!'

The word *Aprille* illustrates both the English knowledge of Latin, by the restoration of the *p* to the Old French loan word (Latin *Aprilem* had become Old French *Avrill*, with *p* becoming *v* before *r*) and also indicates when the flowers used to open in Rome. The word—another time-marking device—derives from a stem meaning 'to open.'

The *soote*, related to Modern English *sweet*, goes back to Indo-European *swād-. With the regular Grimm's Law sound change by which Indo-European *d* became Germanic *t* and with the regular Germanic shift of Indo-European *ā* to *ō*, one gets *swōt-* which evolved either to *sōt-* (spelled *soot-* in Middle English) with the loss of *w* before *ō* (seen also in Old English *swā*, a form that became later English *so*), or to *swēt-* (spelled with two *e*'s in Middle English) if a high front vowel followed, a process seen in Old English *fōt* (Modern *foot*) singular versus *fēt* (Modern *feet*) plural from earlier *fōt-i. The Latin *persuādēre* 'persuade,' from which we get the English *persuade*, rests on this base plus the prefixed morpheme *per* that had an intensifying function seen also in the cognate English *for-* as in *forlorn* 'utterly lost.' Thus the Latin word meant 'to make something very sweet'—the original significance of the compound.

One could extract a great many other facts from this one line, but it should be evident by now how much of one's history is fossilized in the language one uses. A *full* treatment of even the first sentence would require a book in its own right.

NOTES

No single volume can serve as a source book for the type of analysis illustrated in this section. Any good grammar of the relevant period (Middle English) or history of the English language would provide the facts on which the geographical analysis of the line from Chaucer rests. One such text is

Samuel Moore, *Historical Outlines of English Sounds and Inflections,* revised by Albert H. Marckwardt (Ann Arbor, Michigan: George Wahr Publishing Co., 1966), from which the dialect map is adapted. A book which deals with the earlier period (Indo-European to Germanic) would be necessary for relating the English words to their Indo-European antecedents and thence to the various cognates. A standard reference is Albert C. Baugh, *A History of the English Language* (Second Edition; New York: Appleton-Century-Crofts, Inc., 1957).

General treatises on Indo-European are K. Brugmann and B. Delbrück, *Grundriss der Vergleichenden Grammatik der indogermanischen Sprachen* (Second Edition; Strassburg, 1897-1911) and A. Meillet, *Introduction à l'étude comparative des langues indo-européennes* (Seventh Edition; Paris, 1934). Once a word or stem has been traced back to its Indo-European source, the list of roots and stems in dictionaries such as the *Vergleichendes Worterbuch der indogermanischen Sprachen,* edited by A. Walde and J. Pokorney, can be employed to work out or identify the cognates in other branches of Indo-European. Obviously each problem would require the appropriate dictionaries or grammars. Since there are thousands of known languages (see Section 10), a full listing of the available reference works would far exceed the scope of the present book. In each instance, though, synchronically oriented works dealing with the specific period pertinent to the utterance-segment to be analyzed yield one kind of data. Historical grammars enabling one to trace the elements back to a source from which other forms also derive provide the background to the comparative-historical reconstruction.

2. CHRONOLOGICAL RECONSTRUCTION

Linguistic dating procedures group into a number of discrete, crosscutting classificational schemes which rest on *(a)* the types of material handled and the approaches and restrictions associated with each, *(b)* the degrees and types of accuracy inherent in the approaches and materials, and *(c)* the types of perspective desired or obtainable.

One major analytic dichotomy depends on whether the languages under consideration descend historically from a single parent stock or whether they are, insofar as may be known, unrelated to each other. The most well known of the genetic reconstructive techniques—although not the only one—is the glottochronological (also called *glottochronometrical*). Section 2.33 will deal with this. Agenetic techniques can be applied to cognate languages, but their use does not depend on the genetic relationship. The major focus of this entire section on chronology will be that of the agenetic versus genetic considerations.

Another classificational focus differentiates absolute versus relative chronologies. That is, sometimes one can pin a precise calendrical date to a given datum; at other times one can only say that an event took place before or after another event but not precisely when the other event occurred. The usefulness of the latter information varies. Even when one linguistic approach allows only a sequential type of dating, other types of information—linguistic or nonlinguistic—may allow an absolute time to be assigned to one or another of the sequentially fixed events. Furthermore, dating may be either *(a)* uniterminal (or open-ended) or *(b)* biterminal. The biterminal dating would place boundaries on both sides of an event: that is, it must have taken place before one event but after another. The limits of accuracy then would depend in part on how close the two boundaries were.

A different classificational scheme, but one related to that just mentioned, would depend on whether the information sought is purely temporal or whether the chronology itself is simply a way of sorting out and gaining perspective about different varieties of data. The latter type leads to developmental chronologies of selected fields or even of entire cultural systems. This division of the book, particularly Section 2.3, will give some notion of the method, but later sections will fill in more specialized and refined reconstructive techniques.

2.1 Agenetic Considerations

2.11 Simple Dating Procedures

Agenetic techniques are relatively easy to interpret. If one knows, say, that Alexander Fleming discovered penicillin on a particular day and that he gave the antibiotic its name then, one can reliably date all texts containing the word *penicillin* from that period on. However, unless the word should be dropped from the language, the fact that it appeared in a text would give only the earliest possible date for the writing of that text. Furthermore, even if the word should be discontinued, its presence in a text would not necessarily guarantee that the text dated from before the general dropping of the word from the language since occasionally speakers of a language may deliberately employ archaic or obsolete words as a stylistic device. Of course, if a word should become obsolete by a given date, the presence of that word in a text should instantly alert the analyst to the likelihood that the document antecedes that specific time—a fact which may be subject to confirmation by other information.

The foregoing example illustrates a *lexical* coinage which can provide a reference point. In a similar fashion, a *loan word* from one language to another may serve the same function if the date of the foreign influence is ascertainable. A rather simple example would be the fact that no loan word from any American Indian language could have entered a language of the Indo-European group before the speakers of that family (e.g., Italian, Spanish, Portuguese, French, or English) actually encountered the speakers of American Indian languages. Thus the presence of words such as *teepee, squaw,* or *wigwam* in a text would necessarily prove that the document was written after such contact had been established.

Agenetic dating procedures do not rest on lexical evidence alone. Any change in a linguistic system—if observable by some means—may provide chronological evidence. For example, around the year 1250, the French language regularly lost the phoneme (minimal relevant sound unit) /s/ when the /s/ was followed by /t/. Thus the early French word *hostel,* dating from before the loss (1250), became *hotel,* a form clearly dating from after 1250. (The French later indicated this loss by the use of a circumflex accent over the vowel preceding the *t.*) The English borrowed this particular word at two separate times, once before the loss (i.e., the *hostel* variant) and once after it (i.e., the *hotel* variant). A study of such words would indicate something of the chronology of the English-French cultural contact without any need to resort to nonlinguistic criteria.

The loss of the *s* in *hotel* reveals the earliest date at which the word could have been borrowed, but it does not provide the terminal date. This information is not necessarily lacking, but, when it exists, it rests on criteria other than the foregoing. That is, a given word in which the original preconsonantal *s* has disappeared—a fact which would place it as a loan *after* 1250—might not show some other change which took place at a later period of French. Alternatively, it might well show a form indicating that it entered English before some English sound change took place, as attested by the fact that the word underwent the English change—hence must already have been in that language at the time of the change.

One should note that whatever criterion serves as the basis for a relative chronology, normally the same feature (say, the loss of *s,* as here) extends across many items of the language (consider for instance, English *forest* versus post-1250 French *forêt,* or English *feast* beside the French *fête*). If, as in this example, the differential items are loans, an analysis of the entire group of items (here words) by a relative chronology would provide an index of both the nature and extent of the cultural contacts of each period represented. In later sections, I will return to a more systematic treatment of this analytical technique.

2.12 Reconstruction of the History of Fields or Influences

As indicated, later sections will consider more esoteric linguistic techniques for reconstructing history and also prehistory. Sometimes, however, even the most obvious facts (e.g., as in Poe's "Purloined Letter") lie open to view but escape attention, although these facts can provide precisely the informative insights being sought. One simple technique can well serve as the basis for a thorough history in its own right, but one which may deal with any particular field. For at least some languages, such as English, very extensive lexicographic projects have, within reasonable limits, identified the absolute date of the first use of every word in the language as well as the developing changes of meaning of each word down through the centuries. Thus, for instance, in 1878 the enormous organization that was to record the lexicon of the English language on historical principles started gathering the gigantic collection of materials to be used. Veritable armies of researchers were signed on for the task—namely the job of searching all of English writing with the intent of finding the very first use of each and every word. This fantastic project virtually meant the reading and rereading—*ad nauseam* if not *ad infinitum* —of everything ever set down in English. Out of this vast enterprise arose, as by-products, such organizations as the Early English Text Society, dedicated to reprinting out-of-print works, so that these fragments of the total evidence for English use would not be omitted but would be readily available for the workers.

There weren't enough professional linguists in all the world, let alone linguists mad enough to embark on such a seemingly endless enterprise, so every literate or near-literate volunteer was pressed into service—housewives with extra time on their hands, retired school teachers, clergymen, and so on. These volunteer lexicographers, most of them unpaid, lived all over the world— from Australia to South Africa; from America to England. C. T. Unions, one of the editors of the great lexicographic enterprise, has told how he received well-organized, accurate materials over a period of years from one individual whom he had never met personally. One day, finding himself in the man's neighborhood, he impulsively decided to go to meet his ingenious and indefatigable co-worker. When he arrived at the address, he discovered it was that of a mental institution. His story doesn't relate whether the patient was sent to the institution after working on the dictionary for some years or whether he was there before—assuming that it takes a madman to initiate such a thankless job. Nevertheless, in the year 1928—about a half century after the job began—twelve enormous volumes of *The New English Dictionary,* later to be called the *Oxford English Dictionary* after the name of the printing house, issued from the press. A one-volume supplement followed in 1933.

This dictionary listed over a quarter of a million main entries. Of course, there have been larger dictionaries since, but, as suggested, the major innovation was listing the first use, as then known, of every word, with the source in which the word appeared. The great lexicographer Samuel Johnson had also compiled a dictionary based on historical principles (published in 1755), but, as he had worked alone, he had been satisfied merely to attest the use of each word; he had not attempted to identify the firse use as the O.E.D. later did. The achievement of the *O.E.D.* and its competitors (as well as similar projects for other languages) opened an entire approach to historical reconstruction. To the extent that the dictionaries have tracked down the first, or nearly the first, occurrence of each word (at least in written or printed form), one can systematically go through the entire lexicon, noting all of the words used in a given field. Having taken this initial step, one can then arrange the words chronologically. Since the *O.E.D.* and, presumably similar works identify the source of each term, one would then have a listing of the central documents which first presented the new concepts, as well as a compendium of the pioneers in the given field. Even if an analyst had no preconceived idea of what to expect from such a study, its orderly arrangement would, by the very methodology itself, accomplish the following:

(1) Bring together diverse (perhaps long forgotten) data
(2) Sort out the mass of details

(3) Lead unerringly to the sources of the central concepts (which change from period to period)

(4) Provide historical perspective to the whole

The approach, of course, is not entirely foolproof. The *O.E.D.* and the other dictionaries often missed the very first use of words. Furthermore, it is not unreasonable to assume that many words appeared in spoken use for some time before they were first written down. Clearly, words employed by scientists generally occurred in written form sooner after their coinage than words employed by people who normally do not publish the results of their investigations. Yet, even if the analysis errs somewhat because of these factors, it normally does not go too far astray. It is instructive, for instance, to note the fourteenth-century physicians dealing with the bodily "humors" and with astrological or religious concepts in their attempts at therapy. Somewhat later one finds nontechnical terms acquiring a technical meaning. Thus, in 1530 the word *stroke* in the sense of 'brain infarction' appeared in a treatise on pharmacy—one which employed such standard remedies as peacock's dung, unicorn's horn, and so forth—ingredients, one may suppose, readily available at the local apothecary's shop. The use of the word *stroke* itself, although clearly defined by the accompanying description of the syndrome and definitely employed for one of the ailments still described by the same term in customary medical parlance, provides perspective as to the approach of the early sixteenth-century physician. The word, which appears in the phrase "a stroke of God's hand," preserves the inherited Indo-European view of sickness as punishment for sin, an orientation held elsewhere in ancient cultures, but one that is often forgotten by the modern sophisticate. This position, although traceable in many other ways, shows up as just one among the many facts uncoverable in a systematic (and purely mechanical) lexical schematization by chronology. In a similar manner, a parallel study of any field would disclose forgotten or unknown facts, or would buttress and support other information acquired by different means.

If, in addition to grouping the words by conceptual fields, the investigator were to note which words were indigenous to the language and which came from other languages by means of borrowing, he would also have a means of assessing in diachronic perspective the nature and extent of transcultural interaction—of tracing wars, commercial expansion, political interaction, and so on. A later discussion will return to this point. There are two main problems with the rather pedestrian methodology depicted above. The first is purely practical: the approach demands a fantastic amount of preliminary work by the armies of information gatherers required for the reading of absolutely every document ever written. To the extent that the preliminary information is incomplete, the secondary phase—the sorting of the data into accurate sequential form—may lack some precision. Furthermore, no individual investigator could possibly even start his own project in historical reconstruction unless the preliminary phase were already completed. Those analysts who wish to investigate languages which either lack a literary tradition or for which the preliminary investigation—the dating of first or early uses—has not been done cannot employ this approach at all.

A second problem is equally serious or, from some points of view, even more so. The foregoing type of analysis is limited to the period of attested writing. Fortunately, at least some sequential analysis, although not necessarily the kind inherent in the collecting of earlier and later documentation (the procedure just described), can be pursued by different techniques. One can arrive at sequential sorting of the lexicon by means of purely synchronic data. The latter approach will form the subject of later discussion. What should be emphasized here is the central insight that any sequential arrangement of lexicon, however achieved, can provide the basis for the reconstruction of either history or (as will be shown) prehistory.

2.2 Agenetic versus Genetic Considerations

The presence of what looks like the same word in two or more languages may reflect any one of three possibilities:

(1) Common descent from a single ancestral source
(2) Transmission through cultural contract
(3) Sheer chance

Since every language has many thousands of words in its lexicon, in the normal course of events, at least some words are likely to bear random resemblance to words in other languages. How then is one to interpret the surface-level similarity? For example, despite very different orthographic traditions, Greek, Latin, and Sanskrit—three languages which are genetically related and trace their ancestry back to the same Proto-Indo-European source—show strikingly similar forms of the word for 'father,' namely *pater, pater,* and *pitar,* respectively. On the other hand, the proper name *Coca Cola* appears in English, Spanish, and Chibcha (this last, a South American Indian language spoken along the Amazon Valley in Colombia), as well as in many, many other languages. Although English and Spanish are genetically related to each other, Chibcha is not related to the family to which they belong. Clearly, the presence of similar or identical words in these languages does not betoken any common heritage. It simply results from the transmission of cultural ideas and artifacts—including the beverage—from one system to another. Yet how, then, can one distinguish on the basis of such evidence among the three possibilities: genetic relationship, contact of related or unrelated languages, and chance similarity?

The answer lies in a consideration of the total structure of the languages or cultures concerned, not just of the isolated features— here lexical items of surface-level similarity. Observe for example, the following sets of paired terms:

LATIN	ENGLISH
currere 'to run'	*hurry*
cordis 'of the heart'	*heart*
caput 'head'	*head*
canis 'dog'	*hound*

Here, all other factors being equal, every time Latin had a *c* (pronounced k), Germanic, whence eventually English, had an *h*. The relationship, a genetic one, is predictable and consistent. If, on the other hand, one were to find the name *Coca Cola* in Latin, an obvious absurdity since the drink was not known in antiquity, what set of correlations would one have the right to expect under the assumption that the trade name had descended independently into both Latin and English from a common Indo-European source? Obviously, the English "cognate," if there were one, would have to begin with an *h,* and not with a *c.*

It is not an absurdity, of course, to find *Coca Cola* in Spanish or in any other modern language—including Chibcha—since the company concerned sells its products widely. The first sign, for example, that greeted me some years ago when I reached the airport in Cali, Colombia, read, "Tome Coca Cola" ('Drink Coca Cola'). Yet Spanish, the official language of Colombia, derives from Latin. Consequently, it preserves many, though not all, of the same /k/-to-/h/ correlations with English that Latin had (later, in the post-Latin period, secondary sound changes took place.) Thus the Spanish verb *correr* 'to run,' derived from the Latin *currere,* also relates to the English *hurry.*

As seen in the following list, the pattern is more or less regular:

SPANISH	LATIN	ENGLISH
corazon	*cordis*	*heart*
can	*canis*	*hound*
ciento	*centum*	*hundred*
cabeza	*caput*	*head*

Of course the Spanish word *perro* 'dog' has by and large ousted the inherited *can,* and the letter *c* of *ciento* is now pronounced as a fricative (either /θ/ as the *th* of English *thin* or as /s/, the choice depending on the particular dialect of Spanish—normally /s/ in South America) not as a stop (i.e., as a /k/, as it was in Latin.) Nevertheless, in most cases the phonology and in some cases the traditional orthography, which reflects the earlier phonology, attest the inherited relationship. Consequently, an identity such as /k/ (written *c*) in both Spanish and English versions of the name *Coca Cola* does prove something: namely, (*a*) that the word spread by means of transmission and (*b*) that it could not have been inherited from a common Indo-European source.

The Greek, Latin, and Sanskrit words for *father* show a valid set of genetic correlations, not because these words, as words, are similar, but rather because they preserve a set of consistent relationships which may be seen in hundreds of other words (e.g., the *p* in Greek *poús* 'foot,' Latin *pēs* 'foot,' and Sanskrit *pad* 'foot'). On the other hand even apparent dissimilarity can establish a genetic relationship if enough other items preserve the same consistency of patterning. Thus, for instance, the Indo-European *p* became *f* in Germanic (whence English), but it disappeared in the Celtic branch of Indo-European (as in Old Irish). English and Old Irish cognates of the *pater, pater, pitar* group, accordingly, show *father* and *athir*. The fact that this set of correlations (Greek *p*, Latin *p*, Sanskrit *p*, but Germanic *f* and Old Irish zero) is a regular pattern appears demonstrable from many other words, viz., Latin *piscis* 'fish' to English *fish*—earlier *fisc*—and Old Irish *iasc*. Thus the ultimate proof or disproof of any hypothesis concerning relationships must stand or fall on the consistency of the *set* not merely on the apparent similarity of individual items. Sometimes structural considerations of a more deep-seated type may play a role in distinguishing among the genetic, agenetic, or chance similarities, but a later section will deal with these, since they require a bit of background for ready comprehension.

2.3 Genetic Dating

In Mark Twain's novel *A Connecticut Yankee in King Arthur's Court,* the Demoiselle Alisande La Carteloise presents herself before the Round Table with a request for assistance in freeing forty-five beautiful young girls, mainly princesses, from the captivity imposed on them by three ogres, "each with four arms and one eye." When, in his royal kindness, Arthur assigns the task to the Connecticut Yankee, the latter undertakes to ascertain the location of the castle where the maidens are being held.

". . . where is the castle?"

"Oh, as to that, it is great, and strong, and well beseen, and lieth in a far country. Yes, it is many leagues."

"*How* many?"

"Ah, fair sir, it were woundily hard to tell, they are so many, and do so lap the one upon the other, and being made all in the same image and tincted with the same color, one may not know the one league from its fellow, nor how to count them except they be taken apart, and ye wit well it were God's work to do that, being not written man's capacity; for ye will note . . . ."

The rest of the details provided by the noble lady need not concern us beyond the observation that cartographers do draw up maps which bear some relationship, however remote, to the terrain represented. Yet how do such scholars segment or take apart this geography so as to perform their task, particularly when, as Alisande put it, it is "all in the same image and tincted with the same color . . . "? The answer, of course, is that some distinction such as topographic features (e.g., rivers, mountains, etc.) are imposed by nature; others, such as political boundaries, are arbitrary but nonetheless definable in a nonsubjective way; while still others, such as measurement into leagues or miles or kilometers or feet, represent arbitrary choices, which, once fixed, may also be employed in a nonarbitrary way. The choice, however, as to whether to mark individual castles or monuments or wells or any other paticurlar feature may depend on the purpose of the mapmaker.

In the same manner, the problem of periodic division of linguistic materials exists for the "cartographers" of language.

2.31 Sequential Splitting and Comparative Methodology

Change is the norm for language. As will be shown in a later section of this book, linguistic evolution is for the most part directed toward efficiency, but often efficiency may be attained in various ways. Thus, given an unstable structure of almost any kind, different modes of change can take place within that system. If the speakers of a language should separate into subgroups which subsequently migrate apart, the changes in the language of Group A and those in the language of Group B would not necessarily be the same. Indeed, it is inevitable that within a short time each change would beget others, and so the process of differentiation would progress until the two groups spoke mutually unintelligible languages. This differentiation provides a natural line of demarcation for setting up linguistic periods. There is nothing arbitrary about whether or not a change has occurred: either the equivalent forms in the genetically related but now separate languages are identical or they are different. If they are different, the particular feature (or features) by which they dissimilate is the clearcut evidence which marks the split. Had the groups remained together, the same change (or changes) might have taken place anyway, but then both groups would have shared this feature (or these features).

For example, English traces back in an unbroken, graded continuum to a Proto-Indo-European source language, which itself derives from even more remote origins. Just as for Alisande's topographic problem, each segment—here a chronological segment—shades imperceptibly into the next without differential labels. Human beings impose the labels on the material. However, if one considered only the comparative materials which differ, one would be forced to conclude that a series of separations had taken place in the following sequence:

(1) Indo-European
(2) Germanic
(3) West Germanic
(4) Low West Germanic
(5) Anglo-Frisian
(6) Old English

The segmentation into these divisions is neither an arbitrary nor a capricious one. It rests on measurable and readily verifiable criteria —among others, the following.

(1) INDO-EUROPEAN TO GERMANIC

A comparison of any of the Germanic languages with other Indo-European languages discloses the fact that the Germanic group underwent the sound changes formulated under Grimm's Law (see Section 4.11), whereas no other Indo-European language did— although Armenian had two developments parallel to the Grimm's Law changes, but lacked the shift of voiceless stops (p, t, k, k^w) to voiceless fricatives (ϕ, θ, χ, χ^w). Germanic also shows an ā-to-ō change (cf. Latin *māter* versus Old Saxon *mōdar* or Old English *mōdor*—Modern English *mother*) and an *o*-to-*a* change (cf. Latin *octo* 'eight' to Old High German or Old Saxon *ahto* or Gothic *ahtau*), not to mention numerous other differential changes.

(2) GERMANIC TO WEST GERMANIC

Among other changes, any single consonant (except *r*) preceded by a short vowel was doubled if a *j* followed it: **satjan > *sattjan* (later to undergo other changes, whence eventually came the Old English *settan*).

(3) WEST GERMANIC TO LOW WEST GERMANIC

This differentiation rests not on the changes undergone from West Germanic to Low West Germanic but rather on those which separated High West Germanic (whence came Old High German) from her sister groups. These are known as the Second Germanic Consonant Shift (Grimm's Law being the first), which accounts for instance, for Old High German *wasser* (with *t > ts > ss*) compared to Old English *wæter*, Modern English *water*.

Each of the periods has its own characteristic differentiae, which represent the divergent developments after the peoples themselves had separated. Needless to say, changes took place on all levels —phonological, morphological, syntactic, lexical, and semantic— although only the phonological is given here.

Linguists can—and frequently do—subdivide each of the foregoing periods into subperiods, grouped according to the time of every individual change. The division given here, however, rests solely on a comparative analysis of features from one genetically related language family or group to another. Further subdivision, although equally nonarbitrary, would have to rest primarily on internal reconstruction within a given language.

Once one has worked out a sequential chronology of the sort indicated above, it becomes possible to assign sequential dates to contacts between different languages via the specification of the changes undergone by loan words from one language to the other.

That is, if the speakers of one language encounter the speakers of another at a given date, they are likely to borrow at least some words. Yet, if these loan words enter the language prior to the occurrence of any sound changes involving one or more phonemes of the word, the phonemes will be affected by those changes and will, therefore, evolve accordingly, although no such mutation will necessarily take place in the source language. For example, the Germanic tribes on the continent encountered Roman merchants. The Latin word for 'merchant' is *caupō*. Since the word was borrowed prior to the Germanic shift of *au* to West Germanic *ēa,* the *au* underwent the shift to *ēa,* whence came Old English *cēap* (Modern *cheap* or, when compounded, *chap,* as in *chapman* 'merchant[man],' through later, secondary sound change; compare also the *hlaupan* of Gothic, an East Germanic language, with the *hlēapan* 'run' of Old English, a West Germanic language—the latter form eventually to evolve to Modern English *leap*). The fact that the word must have been borrowed after the Germanic tribes had separated from the other Indo-Europeans is evident from the treatment of both the initial *k* (written *c* in Latin) and the *p*. Had the borrowing occurred prior to the Grimm's Law developments, the *k* would have passed to *h* and the *p* to *f*. Two later sections of this book will take up the problem of cultural contact again in somewhat greater detail. Here, let it suffice to note that the dating of the contact is a sequential one, and it rests on the comparative methodology.

2.32. Sequential Differentiation and Internal Reconstruction

The sequential chronology discussed in the preceding section was verifiable by the overt differences (phonology, morphology, syntar, lexicon, etc.) found in any two branches of the same genetically related language family or in any two subsystems (commonly called "dialects") of the same language. It rested on the differences in development of the systems once their users had separated and ceased to have regular communication with each other. Now since, as has been pointed out, change is the norm for language, and mutation goes on whether or not the entire group of users of a language remains together, one should be able to work out relative chronolo-

gies on the basis of these changes. The analysis of this type of evolution rests on internal structural considerations, and, therefore, part of the presentation must be delayed until a later chapter of this book deals with the dynamics of language change. A few comments, however, may provide at least some perspective.

Language at all levels (phonological, morphological, syntactic, lexical, etc.) consists not merely of items (the phonemes, the morphemes, the particular arrangements, etc.) but rather of the contrastive relationships of these items with respect to each other. The Neogrammarians of the late nineteenth century concerned themselves predominantly with the isolated and isolable changes of the items. The direction of linguistic analysis shifted drastically when Ferdinand de Saussure, a linguist trained in the Neogrammarian tradition by Neogrammarians, started to see the necessity of considering the entire set of items and their interrelationships at any one time. For example, note the following set of vowels which are arranged in descending order of tongue height (the particular articulatory manipulation used to differentiate these vowels from each other):

/i/ (the vowel of *beat*)
/ɪ/ (the vowel of *bit*)
/e/ (the vowel of *bait*)
/ɛ/ (the vowel of *bet*)
/æ/ (the vowel of *bat*)

If the tongue were lowered slightly from the position normally employed for the /i/, the resulting sound would be identified by an English speaker as /ɪ/ (the vowel of *bit*, not *beat*). Therefore, the native speaker must keep his critical boundaries—here relative heights of the tongue—or else the resultant will convey the wrong message (e.g., *bit*, not *beat*) or no message at all (e.g., *sim*, not *seem*). If, for reasons to be considered, any single item in this structured set should change, either of two major possibilities must ensue: (a) the distinction between two or more items would disappear (e.g., the vowels of *beat* and *bit* would be pronounced alike), or (b) other items would restructure their relative positions in the system with respect to each other (e.g., if /ɪ/ were to rise, the original /i/ might

then shift to a more retracted position or to a diphthongal articulation such as /aɪ/ or else it would differentiate by some other means.) Sometimes a single, well-motivated change in a system may trigger not just one change but rather a whole chain reaction. For example, in a system such as that given here, a change of /æ/ to /ɛ/ might force /ɛ/ to rise to the /e/ position, thus forcing /e/ to rise to the /ɪ/ position and so on. Note that in the last example, the original /e/ would be forced to shift (here /ɪ/) *before* the /ɛ/ phoneme had completely occupied the /e/ slot. If the /e/ failed to rise *prior* to such a shift, the two phonemes (original /ɛ/—now shifted to /e/ —and original /e/, still pronounced as /e/) would merge, never again to be separated.

The hypothetical example given here is, of course, merely a simplification of the type that normally occurs in language. Most vowel systems differentiate and structure on a variety of distinctive features, not just tongue height (e.g., front versus back articulation, length versus lack of length, rounding of the lips versus nonrounding). Nevertheless the structural dynamics can be seen from this oversimplification. In just such a way, when the vowel now pronounced /e/, as in *dame,* approached its present position, it forced the then existing /e/ to shift upward, forcing the next phoneme to shift in its turn.

When one gets a simple chain reaction with no loss in the number of entities in the system, the users of the language never become aware that any change has taken place. Furthermore the historical linguist cannot identify the change by simple internal evidence: he must rely on external criteria to identify the time of the shift, since the old spelling would continue in the documents at his disposal. Prior to the rise of precise descriptive systems for the recording or analysis of articulation, the change of pronunciation would go unrecorded internally. External evidence, of course, is readily available. For example, the vowel changes that resulted in our current articulatory practice differentiated English phoneme– grapheme correlations from those of languages spoken on the European continent. The letter *e,* is still pronounced /e/ (a vowel close to that of *way,* but minus the final diphthongal glide to /ɪ/ in some European nations, but in England and America it is pronounced /i/ (as in *see*). This change (English /e/ to /i/) can be

dated by means of loan words from English to other languages, or the reverse. Since this change is tied in with the entire set of chain reactions, the entire set of changes is datable through the dating of any independent member.

The dating of subtractive developments requires no external evidence—that is, evidence beyond the language in question—at all. As soon as categories have merged, the results become apparent internally. When the merger is a phonological one, this change is seen in two major types of evidence:

(1) Words that once could not rhyme now may do so.
(2) Spelling fluctuates between the norms for the once discrete phonemes.

Thus, for instance, at the end of the Middle English period the vowel of the word *dead,* once quite discrete from that of the word *red,* fell together with the latter vowel. Henceforth it became possible for the words *dead* and *red* to rhyme, as attested in poetry. In regard to the spelling, once the two phonological sources, represented differently in the orthography, had merged, occasional spellings—chiefly by uneducated people—show variation, e.g., *ded* for *dead.* Prior to the standardization of spelling, brought about by the impact of the printing press, such variability appears regularly even in the writing of well-educated people. For example, at the end of the Old English period the diphthong $\bar{e}o$ merged with the simple vowel $\bar{e}$. After this change, one finds the two spellings *people* and *peeple* occurring side by side, although not always in the practice of a particular scribe. Eventually, of course, the orthography became fixed, but the variation was quite noticeable immediately after the change, and still may be seen sporadically to this day.

2.33 Percentile Retention Averaging: Glottochronology

Perhaps the best known but the least understood of the linguistic techniques for arriving at a chronology is that originally formulated by Morris Swadesh, an anthropological linguist, who was chiefly concerned with languages which occasionally show some

similarities but lack a written literary tradition, such as the Amerindian groups. His attention focused on the problem as a result of some deliberations between two of his teachers, Franz Boas and Edward Sapir, regarding a problem which was originally a non-linguistic puzzle: When two geographically separated cultures show similar features, how is one to interpret these identities? Do they arise *(a)* through cultural transmission (e.g., the use of Coca Cola in many parts of the world) or *(b)* through inheritance from a common ancestral source? The answer lies partially in the nature of the similar items (are they likely to have been invented or discovered independently? do they presuppose sequential lines of development, whence the necessity of traces of that development?) and partially in the entire structure of the culture in which they occur. If any given similarity arises from genetic considerations, then the cultures should have preserved other similarities as well.

These and related lines of thought led Swadesh to the following hypothesis: of all the artifacts of a culture—pottery, clothing, and so on—the one most resistant to change is language. Furthermore, certain portions of a language, particularly that which may be regarded as a common-core vocabulary, are more resistant than others. Presumably people everywhere have to eat and drink, hence must have words for such activities. They must have mothers and fathers, arms and legs, and so on; certainly such core items, which may be regarded as universals, would be assumed to exist in the vocabulary of all languages. Other words, such as *igloo* or *walrus, bamboo* or *palm tree, kangaroo* or *boomerang,* are as clearly indigenous to specific cultures as are the items that they describe. Clearly also, although noncore words are subject to fluctuation and change because of changes in the environment, the need for the core words would remain unchanged because these are grounded in the universals of human experience. Accordingly Swadesh drew up a test list of 215 core words, expressing them in English, but adding notes as to the range of meaning of each term he used. He then compared the words having these meanings in early and late phases of each of a number of languages which have a long recorded and well-attested written tradition to see what he would find. The results of his investigations were striking, and, if carefully interpreted, of great significance.

Swadesh—and, later, other investigators who undertook to check his methods and findings—made such comparisons of a number of languages, chiefly those of Indo-European origin, but also including Chinese (a member of the Sino-Tibetan family) and Egyptian (a member of the Afro-Asiatic family). Ideally, he wanted to compare the relative retention rate of the core lexicon within each of the languages over a similar time span. In practice it was not always possible to keep the unit of time constant so Swadesh worked out a simple mathematical formula for converting the retention rates for time spans of more or less than one thousand years into rates for precisely one thousand years:

$$\log r = \log R \div t$$

(where the logarithm of the unit retention equals the logarithm of the retained per cent divided by the number of time units).

Using this formula, various investigators reported the following results:

Languages Compared	Per cent retention per 1000 yrs.
Classical Latin (50 B.C.) to Modern Romanian	77
Old High German (850 A.D.) to Modern	78
Classic Chinese (950 A.D.) to Modern Colloquial North Chinese	79
Latin of Plautus (200 B.C.) to the Modern French of Molière (1650 A.D.)	79
Middle Egyptian (2100-1700 B.C.) to Coptic (300-500 A.D.)	79
Dominican Carib (1650) to Modern	80
Classic Latin (50 B.C.) to Modern Portuguese	82
Koine Greek (250 A.D.) to Modern Cypriote	83
Koine Greek (250 A.D.) to Modern Athenian	85
Classic Latin (50 B.C.) to Modern Italian	85
Old English (950 A.D.) to Modern English	85
Latin of Plautus (200 B.C.) to Spanish (1600)	85

As shown, the retention rate per one thousand years ranged from 77 to 85 per cent, but with heavy clustering around 79 and 85 per cent. The variations were assumed to have arisen from three main sources:

(*a*) normal statistical fluctuation; (*b*) differences in application of the technique by different investigators; and (*c*) defects in the method. The statistical fluctuation, of course, was to be expected. The differences in application of technique may be understood against the background of the method itself.

The usual everyday equivalents of the test items were compared for two stages of each language. If the forms were clearly related although phonologically different because of normal sound change and if the meanings were substantially the same, a plus score was counted, as in the following:

OLD ENGLISH	MODERN ENGLISH
eall	*all* (+)
and	*and* (+)
æsc	*ashes* (+)
æt	*at* (+)

On the other hand, if the meaning had changed substantially or if a different word had replaced the original, a negative score was tabulated:

OLD ENGLISH	MODERN ENGLISH
dēor	*animal* (−)
fūl	*bad* (−)
rind	*bark* (−)

In the foregoing negative tabulations, one may note that Old English *dēor* did remain in the language, but its meaning had evolved from that of 'animal' to that seen in its modern variant, *deer*. Likewise Old English *fūl* (Modern *foul*) and *rind* (Modern *rind*) show semantic shift, with other lexical items filling their earlier function. The problem here lies in the accuracy of identification of the earlier and later meanings (whence there may be a potential difference in the scoring) as well as in the attesting of all of the available synonyms of the different periods.

Attempts to improve the method itself centered primarily on the nature of the list of test items, with different linguists and anthropologists pointing out that some items (e.g., *ice* or *snow*) were culture-specific, not universal, while other scholars were concerned that the size of the list (often reduced through the elimination of some words) be large enough to preclude significant distortion because of minor and unpredictable fluctuation or occasionally lack of available evidence.

Nevertheless, despite the slight variation produced by tinkering, the range of variation—only six percentage points in unit retention per 1000 years (from 79 to 85 per cent) on the original list—did not invalidate the methodology for what may well be its most important application. When comparative linguistic methods show that two languages are genetically related via divergent development from an earlier ancestral language, one may compute the time period of their separate development within the limits of accuracy of the assumed constancy of retention rate. Each language would presumably lose part of the original core vocabulary at approximately the same rate, but the vocabulary lost would not necessarily be the same once the speakers of the languages had separated. Consequently the proportion of the core vocabulary (now cognate, but with divergence in accord with the separate phonological and other developments—e.g., Spanish *padre* versus French *père*) still held in common would be a reflex of the time of separation: the longer the time span, the fewer the cognate items. The time period of that separate development can be computed by the following formula:

$$t = \log C \div 2 \log r$$

(where C is the percent of cognate vocabulary.)

The methodology was worked out from and tested against those languages which have been recorded for both earlier and later periods. As employed, this linguistic technique shows results not very dissimilar to the dating from nonlinguistic criteria, the differences, as suggested, having arisen from variations in the word list and from the individual practice of the investigator. The most important applications, however, occur in the dating of cultures without a written tradition. Through the techniques depicted here, with or without the various refinements that have been advanced, one can tell at least in a rough fashion how long ago various languages diverged—and from this fact infer a presumed divergence of the peoples—and work out at least relative chronologies and family trees, with all of the implications these hold for tracing migrations and prehistoric developments.

It has been argued that the absolute datings are sometimes off, and this criticism is certainly valid. Yet the method has enabled scholars to introduce some time depth into areas which previously allowed no historic nor prehistoric view at all. Surely information that two groups diverged approximately 300 years ago rather than 3000 years ago must be useful, even if the computation is off considerably. It allows the use of other evidence, sometimes nonlinguistic, sometimes linguistic. Occasionally it may suggest what evidence one should seek for confirmation or disproof. If one has other evidence that another group passed through an area at a specific time, one can look for loan words or other means of crosschecking the assumptions.

The severest strictures against the method have stemmed perhaps from those who expected too much. The method is, within limits, reliable for establishing relative chronologies but is less certain for absolute datings despite the revised lists and revised formulas of different sorts. Nevertheless, it does give some overview and time depth which, under controlled conditions, can prove highly useful.

One additional factor may be worth noting. Clearly special conditions—invasions, trade, migration, and so on—may accelerate or slow down lexical change. Yet it has been pointed out that these features average out over the long span. If more lexical items enter a language at a given moment, there are more noncore items then to start disappearing in accord with the regular loss rate, therefore the language will reduce these faster. Thus although fluctuations may be large at any one time, they do not significantly affect the long-range result. Furthermore, as suggested, the *core* items change at a different pace.

NOTES

The Original Test List (November, 1951)

all (of a number), and, animal, ashes, at, back (person's), bad (deleterious or unsuitable), bark (of a tree), to bite, black, blood, to blow (of wind), bone, to breathe, brother, to burn (intrans.), child (young person), clothing, cloud, cold (of weather), to come, to cook, to count, to cry (weep), to cut, to dance, day (opposite of night rather than time measure), to die, to dig, dirty, dog, to drink, dry (substance), dull (as of a knife), dust, ear, earth (soil), to eat, egg, eight, eye, to fall (drop rather than topple), far, fat (organic substance), father, to fear, feather (larger feathers rather than down), few, to fight, fire, fish, five, to float, to fly, fog, foot, four, to freeze, to give, good, grass, green, guts, hair, hand, he, head, to hear, heart, here, to hit, to hold (in hand), how, hundred, to hunt (game), husband, I, ice, if, in, to kill, to know (facts), lake, to laugh, leaf, left (hand), mother, mountain, mouth, name, narrow, near, neck, new, night, nine, nose, not, old, one, other, person, to play, to pull, to push, to rain, red, right (correct), right (hand), river, road (or trail), root, rope, rotten (especially as a log), to rub, salt, sand, to scratch (as with fingernails to relieve itch), sea (ocean), to see, seed, seven, to sew, sharp (as of a knife), to shoot, short, to sing, sister, to sit, six, skin (person's), sky, to sleep, small, to smell (perceive odor), smoke (of fire), smooth, snake, snow, some, to speak, spear, to spit, to split, to squeeze, to stab, to stand, star, stick (of wood), stone, straight, to suck, sun, to swell, to swim, tail, ten, that, there, they, thick, thin, to think, this, thou, three, to throw, to tie, tongue, tooth (front rather than molar), tree, to turn (change one's direction), twenty, two, to vomit, walk, warm (of weather), to wash, water, we, wet, what?, when?, where?, white, who?, wide, wife, wind, wing, to wipe, with (accompanying), woman, woods, to work, worm, ye, year, yellow.

General Reference Works

The particular reference works to be used as analytic tools in chronological reconstruction necessarily differ according to the purpose and the language involved. Because of the great number of languages that exist, no attempt can be made to present a complete bibliographical listing. In general, however, the following types of work may be employed:
  (1) Etymological dictionaries
  (2) Historically dated dictionaries, listing the first uses of words
  (3) Grammars

(4) Histories—particularly phonological histories—of the languages under investigation

Thus, if loan words enter language B from language A, etymological dictionaries would record that fact. A simple examination of the form of the words in both languages would disclose any changes which might serve as the basis for dating the transaction. For example, the French word *forest* entered English, but, since the English version has an *s,* the word must have been borrowed before the French word had lost the *s,* thus becoming Modern French *forêt.* Conversely, the phrase *bête noire* could not have entered English before Old French *beste* (borrowed earlier as *beast*) had lost the *s.* The dictionaries would identify the forms of the words, and linguistic histories of the language concerned, then would provide the absolute (or sometimes relative) dates of entry. The grouping of such loan words by dates or periods would give a reliable index of the nature of the sociocultural interchange.

The dictionaries of the *Oxford English* type, giving the first use of words and the date of that use, provide a basis for reconstructing the history of fields. The analyst, of course, must be alert to the need to utilize the most up-to-the-minute source book. For example, a *Middle English Dictionary* (originally edited by Hans Kurath and Sherman M. Kuhn but now by others) has been in progress for some years, appearing fascicle by fascicle. At least some of the *OED*'s datings have been superseded by earlier material uncovered in the *MED*'s citations.

Almost any reasonably complete and accurate dictionaries, not just etymological or historical ones, can serve as the basis of genetic analyses, either of the glottochronological kind (which would check out the number of retained core-vocabulary words for the purpose of computing estimated times of separation of related groups) or of the protolexical reconstructive kind. More will be said in later sections about the latter possibility.

Specialized Readings on Glottochronology

Carroll, John B., and Isidore Dyen. "High Speed Computation of Lexicostatistical Indices," *Language,* 38 (1962), 274-278.

Cowan, H. K. J. "A Note on Statistical Methods in Comparative Linguistics," *Lingua,* 8 (1959), 233-246.

Dyen, Isidore. "The Lexicostatistical Classification of the Malayopolynesian Languages," *Language,* 38 (1962), 38-46.

———. "The Lexicostatistically Determined Relationship of a Language Group," *International Journal of American Linguistics,* 28 (1962), 153-161.

———. "Lexicostatistically Determined Borrowing and Taboo," *Language,* 38 (1962), 60-66.

———. *A Lexicostatistical Classification of the Austronesian Languages.* Supplement to *International Journal of American Linguistics,* Vol. 31, No. 1 (1965).

Ellegard, Alvar. "Statistical Measurement of Linguistic Relationship," *Language*, 35 (1959), 135-156.

Elmendorf, W. W. "Lexical Innovation and Persistence in Four Salish Dialects," *International Journal of American Linguistics*, 28 (1962), 85-96.

———. "Lexical Relation Models as a Possible Check on Lexicostatistic Inferences," *American Anthropologist*, 64 (1962), 760-770.

Fairbanks, Gordon H. "A Note on Glottochronology," *International Journal of American Linguistics*, 21 (1955), 116-124.

Gudschinsky, Sarah C. "Lexico-statistical Skewing from Dialect Borrowing," *International Journal of American Linguistics*, 21 (1955), 138-149.

———. "The ABC's of Lexicostatistics (Glottochronology)," *Word*, 12 (1956), 175-210.

Hirsch, David I. "Glottochronology and Eskimo and Eskimo-Aleut Prehistory," *American Anthropologist*, 56 (1954), 825-838.

Hockett, Charles F. "Linguistic Time-Perspective and Its Anthropological Uses," *International Journal of American Linguistics*, 19 (1953), 146-152.

Lees, Robert B. "The Basis of Glottochronology," *Language*, 29 (1953), 113-127.

Swadesh, Morris. "Diffusional Cumulation and Archaic Residue as Historical Explanations," *Southwestern Journal of Anthropology*, 7 (1951), 1-21.

———. "Mosan I: A Problem of Remote Common Origin," *International Journal of American Linguistics*, 19 (1953), 26-44.

———. "Comment on Hockett's Critique," *International Journal of American Linguistics*, 19 (1953), 152-153.

———. "Time Depths of American Linguistic Groupings: With Comments by G. I. Quimby, H. B. Collins, E. W. Haury, G. G. Ekholm, and Fred Eggan." *American Anthropologist*, 56 (1954), 361-377.

Taylor, Douglas, and Irving Rouse. "Linguistic and Archeological Time Depth in the West Indies," *International Journal of American Linguistics*, 21 (1955), 105-115.

3. GEOGRAPHICAL RECONSTRUCTION

Within limits to be specified, linguistic evidence can provide the following kinds of geographical information:

(1) Clear-cut proof that two or more languages widely separated in space or time are genetically related, hence that the ancestral parent language was spoken in a single area prior to the dispersal of the users of the language

(2) Information about the environment in which the ancestral language was spoken (e.g., the flora, the fauna, the climate, etc.), hence a potential means for pinpointing the original homeland, regardless of where the speakers later migrated

(3) Information about the path taken by the migrating peoples and where they stopped en route

(4) Information about ancient contacts between the speakers of different languages

(5) Information about the geographical origin and travels of any single individual, ancient or modern

(6) Information about the different people who have resided in a given area, regardless of whether they still live there or not

(7) Information about the original topography of a region, even if some of the features have changed (e.g., if the rivers have dried up, or if the forests have been cut down, etc.)

Some of the reasoning behind the foregoing assertions has already appeared; other information or techniques will appear in later sections of this work, but the presentation will be postponed here, either for strategic purposes (i.e., for the build-up of the background necessary for easy comprehension) or for convenience. Therefore the immediately following sections will support only some of the major points asserted above.

3.1 Genetic Relationships

The types of proof necessary to establish genetic relationships among languages has already been given in part. More will appear later. It should suffice here merely to emphasize the need for a precise statement of phoneme-to-phoneme correspondence, with sufficient morphological and lexical evidence to support the assumption of descent from a common source. The major requirement is that of consistency of patterning, not of superficial similarity, no matter how close the similarity may be. Chance similarities inevitably appear in all languages. Only when a similarity (or even dissimilarity) appears with great regularity does it carry weight as evidence. Sometimes, however, even a few random examples may be convincing if they display a structural principle or pattern attested elsewhere in a system. Thus if there is substantial evidence that several voiceless stops became voiceless fricative, even a couple of examples of another correlation between a different voiceless stop and a voiceless fricative would be important, since it would support the major patterning. It may be asserted here—and discussed in a later section—that fundamental parameters and not just details of a system change (e.g., stop versus fricative articulation).

It should be realized that the current speakers of a given language are not necessarily the genetic descendants of the speakers of the ancestral source language. Thus, for example, many Americans of African ancestry now speak English, a language remotely derived from Indo-European, not from any of the major language families of Africa. Obviously the ancestors of the Afro-Americans, mostly brought to the United States as slaves, gave up their ancestral language and learned that of their new masters—carrying over traces of their original tongue, of course. In a similar fashion, the descendants of aborigines originally encountered by the English speakers likewise adopted the language of the latter group, giving up their native Micmac, Menomeni, and so on. Nevertheless, the presence of a language even thousands of miles from its nearest relative implies (a) a continuity of culture and (b) that at least some of the descendants of the original speakers were involved in the transmission and migration of the language. This type of evidence, however, must be used with caution and should be subject to additional analysis, linguistic or otherwise. For example, if a North American of African origin—now a speaker of English—were to move to Africa or South America, the presence of an English speaker amidst the speakers of African languages or of Spanish or Portuguese would not mean that a descendant of the proto-Indo-Europeans had migrated to another continent. The foregoing facts mean neither that a genetic linguistic relationship is to be equated directly with a genetic nonlinguistic relationship, either physical or cultural, nor that the genetic linguistic relationship is to be ignored. Taken together with other evidence it can be a source of valuable information.

3.2 The Primal Homeland

If words exist in different branches of a genetically related language family and if they can be shown by regular comparative procedures (i.e., phoneme-to-phoneme correlation, etc.) to have descended from the same source word, certain consequences arise. First of all, these words must have signified meanings of relevance to the speakers of the protolanguage. People do not use meaning-bearers unless they think about or discuss the meanings in question. Certainly a reconstruction of the protolexicon can provide a key to at least the topics of their thoughts and discussions although perhaps not to the details of their lucubrations. The problems of dealing with all or part of such a lexicon will provide the focus for Section 4, but here one may note the usefulness, both negatively and positively, of at least part of the lexicon for the reconstruction of the primal homeland where the ancestors of many of the later speakers of languages once resided.

Negative Evidence. None of the Eskimo-Aleut group of languages possesses any words for 'palm tree,' 'banana,' or 'kangaroo.' Conversely the Austronesian languages lack words for 'snow,' 'ice,' and 'polar bear.' These gaps—except as occasionally filled out by loan words when the ideas themselves reach the peoples—are not haphazard nor random. The inhabitants of the Arctic regions, never having seen nor heard about flora and fauna found in tropical or semitropical climates, have no need for lexical manifesting units to deal with the nonexistent (to them) conceptual spheres. In the same way, the ideas of ice or snow or other characteristics of frigid areas require no lexical focus for people in tropical environments.

Yet this very fact makes the lack of certain words every bit as meaningful for reconstructive purposes as the presence of other words. To be sure, occasionally a traveler will tell stories of far-off places with strange and alien characteristics; given such travelers, one may well expect to find loan words creeping into the home system. Such borrowings, identifiable as such by any of a variety of means—including nonnative phonology, nonnative morphology, lack of proper phoneme-to-phoneme correlation in different members of the language group, and so on—hold no significance for the reconstruction of the ancestral homeland except in a negative way: lack of words assignable to the ancient protolanguage reflect the corresponding lack of the concept for the earlier period.

To be sure, individual languages of a group may develop words to fit the new conditions in which the speakers find themselves, but innovations of this kind would be lacking in other languages of the same family; hence the coinages would not be attributable to the protolexicon. Thus, for example, although at least some loans and some post-Indo-European coinages appear in all Indo-European languages, none of these words permit any reconstruction of the ancient vocabulary, and this very lack immediately provides negative triangulation for ruling out specific areas as the ancestral homeland. For instance, the fact that no Indo-European words (i.e., those descended from antiquity) for 'elephant,' 'monkey,' or 'fig' can be reconstructed rules out India as the potential source. Lack of Indo-European words for 'donkey,' 'lion,' and 'camel' rules out Iran. Lack of words for 'olive,' 'cypress,' and so on rule out those areas bordering on the Mediterranean.

This negative delimitational technique does not by itself necessarily indicate where the original speakers did live, but it does rule out many possibilities. There is no necessity, of course, that the "urheimat" was an area in which any Indo-European-derived language is still spoken, but the general geographical distribution on the whole family does suggest such a likelihood. Of greater consequence, the negative evidence—lack of certain lexical items—dovetails with and thus reinforces the positive evidence. Systematic analysis of all negative evidence rules out any areas south of the Black Sea or north of the Baltic, and it further restricts the range to Europe.

Positive Evidence. The foregoing type of negative evidence ruled out certain areas. The positive evidence, which consists of the lexicon assignable to the protolanguage, must agree with the negative. Actually one does not need a great deal of evidence to pinpoint the territory in question. Just as we saw that only a few samples were required for the assignment of Chaucer's home to the Southeast Midland area of England, so too, in a similar fashion, a few words suffice to do this job. Additional analysis merely corroborates the assumptions made. Thus an Indo-European stem * *laks-*, 'salmon,' seen in German *lachs,* Swedish *lachs,* Tocharian *laksi,* and so on, immediately fixes our region as that surrounding the rivers emptying into the Baltic and North Seas. Another Indo-European stem, *$*b^h\bar{a}g$-* 'beech tree,' further confines the homeland to central or north-central Europe, but places a limit on the range, since beech trees appear no farther east than Poland and the Ukraine. The Scandinavian countries (i.e., a northwest boundary) fall outside the range since Indo-European possessed a word for 'turtle,' not found in Scandinavia. Just these words—further supported by a few others—would suggest a territory near the modern rivers Elbe, Oder, and Vistula. The entire range of reconstructable lexicon confirms the deduction. All of the major fauna and flora, which non-linguistic evidence shows once existed from the late Stone Age down to the Bronze Age in the Baltic and North German plains, find corresponding Indo-European words, including those for additional trees such as the 'birch' and the 'aspen'; predatory animals such as the 'bear,' 'wolf,' 'fox,' and 'weasel'; insects such as the 'bee' (and associated terms like 'honey'), 'hornet,' 'wasp,' and 'flea'; birds such as the 'eagle,' 'crane,' 'owl,' 'falcon,' and so forth. It would take a full volume to go through the list or to analyze the phonology and morphology so as to show the reasoning behind the reconstructions. What is central here is the recognition of the total coherence of the pattern. Although one may suggest the picture on the basis of a few shreds of evidence, the overwhelming mass of data which supports the assumption must carry weight.

3.3 The Path of Migration

Although the speakers of some languages may still reside in the very same region in which their remote forebears lived, contrary to modern—and perhaps nationalistic—views, such a situation is extremely rare at least if one traces the pattern back far enough. Since every genetically related family of languages presupposes an original homeland, which a relatively homogeneous group of people speaking a mutually comprehensible dialect once inhabited, the geographical spread of such linguistic systems must establish the fact that at least most of the related languages have been carried far from their primal source. The Austronesian group, for example, consists of no less than five hundred related languages spread across the islands of the Pacific and Indian Oceans, extending from Madagascar to Easter Island in an east-to-west range, and from Formosa to New Zealand in a north-to-south extension, not to mention innumerable minor but isolated areas beyond this enormous stretch. If, as seems clear, this group started from some original point, the speakers of the later divergent patterns had to travel far.

In a similar fashion, the Indo-European family has spread considerably beyond its original domain, having been carried to Australia, India, and North America, as well as to so many other places not even on the European continent to which it may be traced. Even English, a single subbranch, did not arrive in the British Isles until 449, as indicated by statements found in the *Anglo-Saxon Chronicles* and further supported by linguistic evidence. The Celtic tribes were already there when Hengest and Horsa, the chieftains of the West Germanic warriors who crossed the Channel to become the ancestors of the English, first disembarked in their future home. Yet, even keeping in mind the caution regarding the noninterchangeability of language and race (mentioned in an earlier section), there is every likelihood that the ancestors of both the Celts and the Germanic groups, not to mention the Indo-Iranians, Armenians, or other subgroups of the family, set out from the same geographical starting point. Can one trace the path of these migrations so many centuries—

even millennia—afterwards? The answer is a qualified yes! Sometimes one can, although the analysis occasionally requires a bit of
technology behind it, not to mention a fair bit of luck. Section 3.6
will deal with the systematic analysis of place names (toponyms) for
the disclosure of the various groups which have resided in any given
area. Often enough, when a large group migrated in antiquity, it
stopped for varying periods in different areas—at least long enough
to place its own stamp on the descriptive epithets of the places. Thus,
for example, the Celtic tribes migrated not only clear across Europe,
but they even passed through Asia Minor at some remote time to
leave the name *Galatoi* on some of their descendants. They passed
through Italy at another period, leaving behind the name *Medio-
lānum* (later *Milan*), from *medio-* 'middle' plus *lānum* 'flatland'
(earlier **plānum*), which shows the regular Celtic loss of Indo-
European **p* (cf. *athir* for **patēr* 'father' or *iasc* for **piskis*). The
Dan- of *Danube* is a Celtic word for 'river.' In such a manner one
may follow the path of the wanderers from place name to place
name. Whenever they stopped for any length of time they left fragments of their language behind in the form of geographical labels—
lexical calling cards, as it were.

For many years the *-ass-* formative of many Greek toponymics
puzzled classical scholars, who recognized the element as non-Greek
in origin although it appears frequently enough in ancient toponymics. Recently L. R. Palmer has suggested that the Indo-European
-osy- adjectival element regularly became *-ass-* in ancient Luvian,
an Indo-European language of the Anatolian subgroup (a dialect
closely related to Hieroglyphic Hittite). With the recognition of this
fact, certain other previously unanalyzable linguistic elements begin
to make sense. For example, the *Parn-* of *Parnassos,* the site of the
ancient Greek temple, quite literally means 'temple' in Luvian. The
implications of this and other evidence of the same kind suggest
the possibility that the Luvians had passed through Greece prior to
the arrival of the Greeks themselves. Naturally this assumption as
well as others which rest on the same type of evidence must be
subjected to the test of additional analysis, nonlinguistic as well as
linguistic. If the Luvians actually were there at one time, it seems
reasonable to assume that they would have left some traces other

than just names behind. The linguistic evidence, therefore, should stimulate investigators to pursue this line of inquiry, but ought not to stand by itself without considerable confirmation.

One must, of course, carefully guard against placing too much credence in isolated and irregular facts. Nevertheless one may always take evidence where one finds it, with a view to subsequent proof or disproof of any hypothesis based on such facts. For example, a certain amount of botanical evidence points to some kind of ancient connection between Polynesia and certain portions of the western coast of South and Central America. Whether there was a single migration from the American continent to Polynesia or the reverse—or whether there may have been regular round trips— remains as yet unestablished. Scholars are still arguing the point. Botanically the direction from America to Polynesia seems more likely. However, the specific plants in question, such as the sweet potato and particular varieties of (normally) cultivated cotton, are found only in Polynesia and the Americas. The Polynesian word for 'sweet potato' is *kumara* in Hawaian, and closely related (and pre-dictable) variants of the same form appear in other Polynesian languages. Since an Ecuadorian Quechua word for the same plant is *kumar* (spelled *cumar* by the nineteenth century botanist who first recorded the word), much has been made of the similarity.

Normally such an isolated item would be discounted by linguists (of the non-lunatic-fringe variety), but the addition of the botanical connection, which seems certain and demands an explanation involving human transmission of the plants, raises this particular lexical correspondence to a level calling for serious examination. A few other possible lexical correspondences are also worth study, although acceptance of the correlations either as loan words or as cognates requires more substantive proof. Just as in the example given earlier of the few lexical equations—which become more plausible and even likely although unsupported by other identities of the same kind, provided they fit into a general pattern of correlations—the isolated examples of the *kumara*-type do not stand or fall by themselves. They too rest on the concept of patterning.

In this instance a potential assumption of a genetic relationship between Quechua and languages of the Austronesian family must be denied unless substantial numbers of vocabulary items should be adduced showing a regular set of phonological correlations. Likewise, the lack of more than a few possible loans precludes the likelihood of any prolonged cultural contact with frequency of migration and communication in either direction. Thus the few lexical correlations would seem to represent more than accidental similarity because of the combination of both botanical and linguistic identity, yet the purely linguistic evidence suggests that the ancient contact of the peoples involved was sporadic and limited at best. There was no genetic relationship, nor was there mass migration or trade. At most, a few boats from one group crossed the seas, and the speakers of one language, bringing with them the *kumara* and a few other tokens of their own homeland, settled down in a distant land, soon to adopt the language and customs of their new home. Only the sweet potato and the other relics of the ancestral land, together with a few of the words which described these relics, remained to attest the transaction and its consequences.

3.4 Ancient Contacts

The example of the *kumara/kumar* equation (in Section 3.3) illustrated the migration of a microsegment of a population, as well as an ancient contact, though a limited one. Any systematic examination of loan words, however, necessarily discloses bicultural interaction. Furthermore, as already suggested in Section 2, one can readily assign these loans to their appropriate time-depths, by applying one technique or another, and thus work out the history of the contact of the systems in question. For instance, such a procedure would reveal the following sequence, among others, for the English or their remote ancestors:

(1) Contact between the Germanic tribes and the Romans before the tribes migrated from the European continent to England (i.e., prior to 449)

(2) Contact between the Germanic and the Celtic tribes in England (after 449)

(3) The impact of the Roman Catholic missionaries (e.g., St. Augustine and followers) on the Old English tribes in the late sixth and the early seventh centuries

(4) Three successive stages of impact of Scandinavian invaders (Vikings) on the late Old English peoples, from the seventh to the eleventh centuries

(5) The second major impact of the Roman Catholic Church on England, this interaction having taken place in the tenth century stemming from the Benedictine Reform movement

(6) The impact of Norman French on England in two stages, the more important one being that from the mid-thirteenth century on, reflecting a decree of 1244 by which owners of property in both England and France had to relinquish their possessions in one country or the other, thus making the nobility subject to either the French or the English king, but not to the two monarchs simultaneously, a situation that had been causing divided and often conflicting loyalties.

Each of the foregoing stages, as well as later ones which can be identified, would emerge simply by a straightforward analysis of loan words borrowed into English. These loans, even in their later forms, provide direct evidence for both the time and the precise nature of the transcultural interactions. Thus, as already noted, the English word *cheap* attests in modern form the ancient contacts of pre-English Germanic tribes with Roman merchants. The nature of the commerce that took place so long ago appears in the words for actual items of trade, such as *wine* or *cheese,* which trace back to the Latin *vīnum* (the Latin *v* was pronounced as a /w/ at that time) and *cāseus*. The fact that the words date back to that particular period rather than to earlier or later periods is unmistakably clear from the particular sound changes that the Latin words had to undergo in order to take the form they now have in English (e.g., *cāseus* > **kæsi* > **čæsi* > **čēasi* > **čiese*—the last form written *ciese* in Old English—and so on). Still other words attest the Germanic contacts with the Roman military organization that used to build paved roads (Latin *strātae viae,* whence we get English *street*), measure their daily marches in thousands of steps (Latin *mīlia passuum,* whence comes English *mile*), and so forth.

In like fashion, one sees that the first contact of the Old English people with the Scandinavians reflected warfare conducted in raids from the sea (e.g., the Old English borrowings—many dropped during later stages of English—*barda* 'ship with a beaklike prow,' *cnearr* 'small warship,' *batswegen* 'boatswain,' *orrest*, 'battle,' *dreng* 'warrior'), whereas the third contact period, that resulting from the Scandinavians' having settled down and intermarried in England, reflects such extensive and profound interaction that the list of loans ranges across the whole spectrum of daily activity and is exceedingly long.

Additional details need not concern us here since the purpose is to indicate the nature of the methodology, not the history of England. Nevertheless, one may readily see how one could reconstruct the history of any culture by means of lexical and other analysis, even if all nonlinguistic evidence had completely disappeared. Obviously some details would be lost; one could identify the fact of trade with Roman merchants or the invasion of the Scandinavians and the precise time of each without also knowing, say, of the Battle of Brunanburg or the Treaty of Wedmore. However, the main historical outlines and perspective would remain, fossilized in the communicational system itself.

3.5 The Provenience and Travels of the Individual

A later section will deal in a more thoroughgoing way with the problem of identifying by linguistic means the placement of any given individual within the framework of the entire sociocultural setting. The following brief remarks will merely highlight some of the geographical information one can retrieve about a single person through the medium of that person's use of language.

Some years ago Dr. Henry Lee Smith, a specialist in the dialectology of English, had a radio program in which he would first invite a member of the studio audience to read a few test sentences, then would say, for example, that the reader had lived in Philadelphia for twelve years before moving to Boston for three, then New York for the next fifteen, and so on. As with the examples referred to in Section 1, much of his reply was simple showmanship designed to impress the audience. Nevertheless most of his identifications were accurate, although the statements about the time the informants had lived in any area were guesses, not certainties. His analyses represented on a more sophisticated plane exactly what

most native speakers of, say, American English do when they identify
a person as British rather than American, because of the latter's
accent or because of the use of some expression or other element—
e.g., "Everything's tickety-boo"—indigenous to England rather than
America.

The nonlinguist, of course, usually, though not always, rests
his guess on an instinctive or intuitive reaction rather than on a
firm knowledge of what specific features differentiate the patterns.
The linguist does not remain content with his own intuition, which
need not be any more acute than that of the nonspecialist; he merely
knows how to go about identifying the features he needs in order to
pinpoint a person's geographical background. These features exist at
every linguistic level—phonological, grammatical, lexical, and semantic—and even spill over into the gestural systems employed.
Speakers of different varieties of the same language, not to mention
speakers of different languages, wave their hands, cross their legs,
and even nod their heads in ways that characterize their places of
origin.

The easiest and most readily identifiable feature is the simple, geographically limited, lexical item. Even the nonlinguist, of
course, identifies the geographical determinant of *pram, spanner,*
or *petrol,* used in England, as contrasted with the equivalent *baby
carriage, wrench,* and *gasoline* (or *gas*) of American usage. Yet every
little town, subdivision of a city, borough, private school, and so on
has its own "private" and preferred lexical mode. What is called
seesaw in one area is *teeter-totter* in another. The variants *angle
worm, mud worm, fishing worm, angle dog, earth worm,* each has
its specific geographical range. If a person lives all his life in a given
area, he normally uses the vocabulary indigenous to that locale. If
he should move, his lexical choices would reflect each area in which
he had resided. He might show, for example, the lexical variant of
one place in selecting *teeter-totter* but that of another when referring
to the bait for fishing. This bifurcation would be evidence of his
duality of background.

Far more reliable than vocabulary is the totality of one's
phonological pattern. A single word is readily picked up even in a
brief stopover, but characteristic pronunciations are far more deeply
ingrained and are quite difficult to disguise even deliberately.

The identification of a person's geographic background via linguistic evidence is relatively simple. For example, on the basis of just a few frequently recurring features, an analyst can place every speaker of American English first in one of the seven major dialect areas of the United States and then in various subareas. For instance, the loss or weakening of /r/ in preconsonantal position (as in *card* or *start*) characterizes eastern sections of New England (parts of Vermont, Massachusetts, and Connecticut), most of the New York City area, and most of the South (particularly around the coast of South Carolina and the Virginia Piedmont area). The first two sections generally drop this /r/ in word-final position also unless a word beginning with a vowel immediately follows without any pause (as in *far away*), but the southern dialects drop the word-final /r/ (preserved in the standard spelling) even there. All other sections of the country preserve an /r/ both before consonants and finally. Thus the treatment of this one feature alone immediately delimits a speaker's range to a single possibility out of three.

A second feature, the retention of a rounded vowel in words such as *cot* characterizes eastern New England, and separates that area from New York City and its immediate environment. The New Yorker distinguishes *cot* and *caught,* but the man from Boston does not. This same merger of vowels occurs in the West Midland area (western Pennsylvania, western Maryland, parts of West Virginia). Consequently, a speech pattern retaining preconsonantal /r/ but the merger of the vowels of *cot* and *caught* would identify either the southern or the New York City speaker, these two being differentiated on the basis of their treatment of word-final /r/ before words beginning with vowels, as well as by numerous other features not discussed here. Retention of /r/ in all positions with differentiation of the vowels of *cot* and *caught* characterizes a Middle Atlantic area (eastern sections of Pennsylvania, southern New Jersey, northern Delaware, and segments of Maryland). Thus, even a knowledge of the distribution of only two features allows a complex delimitation.

Obviously the geolinguist is not restricted to the two features discussed here. He can find hundreds, perhaps thousands of others. Theoretically, if enough crosscutting features were identified, one should be able to place the individual not merely with respect to his home state or city, but rather even with respect to the very block he inhabits. In practice, of course, no linguists have bothered to make enough observations for the identification of demarcative features to do this.

The techniques and applications of these techniques to the problems of the historian vary with the available data. The geographic placement of an individual—under certain circumstances a matter of potential interest to the historian—presents different complications depending on the period under consideration. In very recent times literacy has been high, and the orthography, quite standardized. Most well-educated individuals spell words alike although they may pronounce them differently. Thus the phonological desiderata just discussed would normally not play any role at all if the only available evidence were written documentation. On the other hand, important historical figures of recent times have appeared on television or radio and their speech patterns have been recorded. Any short utterance should suffice to place the speaker geographically. Obviously longer utterances allow more criteria to be weighed and permit cross-checking of assumptions by additional information. Also longer utterances may disclose more complex patterns of dyssystemic features to reveal that the speaker had formerly resided in more than one geographical area.

Here it might be emphasized that every geographical influence shows up linguistically and that no major influence can ever be completely eradicated. This analyst, who does not regard himself as a specialist in American English linguistic geography, had no difficulty at all in placing the background of one of his colleagues—a speech teacher, who is also one of the world's most perceptive phonologists—despite the fact that the latter had been trying for years to eliminate his own regional linguistic traits. This fact reflects no discredit on the scholar. The complexity of the task, the sheer statistical weight of the number of distinctive features and of the number of combinations or permutations into which they enter, staggers the imagination of anyone who has any familiarity with the problem. One may eliminate a phonological contrast in one place, but the number of items into which that contrast enters makes some slip inevitable, particularly if one is tired or excited. Even if the speaker is alert and careful, he may slip up. Consider, for example, how many words in English have or once had /r/ in preconsonantal or word-final position, how many involve the /ɔ/-/a/ (*caught-cot*) contrast. Normally, of course, the speaker to be analyzed would not be trying to disguise his linguistic pattern. For the most part, it would be highly unlikely that he would even know how much information he would be conveying in his discourse.

For the period before the mechanical recording of sound, the linguistic detective must rely on visual documentation. For those periods prior to the advent of the printing press, with its concomitant standardization of orthography, phonological differentiation is relatively transparent. Some evidence of this type appeared in the Middle English example from Chaucer cited in the first section of this book. Another example would be the tripartite treatment of the present participle in early Middle English, with *-ande* appearing in the Northern dialect, *-ende* in all of the Midland dialects, and *-inde* in both major Southern dialects (that called "Southern"—a continuation of the West Saxon of Old English times—and also the Kentish). Thus any time an author of that period employed a present participle, he immediately identified his place on this threefold north-to-south continuum.

Additional features, such as the verbal endings in the third person, both singular and plural, provide further support for this north-to-south segmentation and also allow additional differentiation of the Midland dialects. For example, the North Midland dialects, both Eastern and Western, employed *-es* in the third person singular as compared with the South Midland dialects, also both Eastern and Western, which used *-eth* (e.g., *talkes* versus *talketh*). Still other features, such as the Middle English treatment of what was Old English *a* before nasal consonants, provides an east-versus-west segmentation. Thus one finds *man* and *rank* in East Midland dialects but *mon* and *ronk* in the West.

A great many other well attested features provide useful diagnostic cues. These include important phonological, morphological, and lexicogrammatic (i.e., closed-system lexical) distinctions. Many specific words, of course, also appear as characteristic features (e.g., Northern *egges* versus Southern *eyren*), but the analyst normally places his greatest reliance on the items of highest frequency of occurrence, those likely to appear in almost every sentence. Each time a speaker used a pronoun of the third person, a necessity in the normal exigencies of speaking or writing, he identified himself as a native either of the Northern or Northeast Midland areas (if he used *them*) or of any other area (if he used *hem*, the ancestor of our Modern English *'em*). He could not avoid making this evidence available as he had to use either one or the other form. On the other hand, with lexical items not belonging to the closed systems the available choices were wider and the likelihood of a diagnostic lexical item's appearing was slight except under restricted circumstances. For instance, most conversations or documents would not be likely to contain the word for *eggs* but a breakfast conversation might. Nevertheless, regardless of the frequency of any one feature, it should be eminently clear that every communication contains evidence of the communicator's provenience.

Mixed patterns—for example, those showing typically non-Northern features, such as *hem* for the third person plural independent pronoun, *-eth* for the third person singular verbal ending, and *-inde* for the participle, plus sporadic items, such as *kirk* or *egges*, reflecting Northern influence—would point to one major habitation (non-Northern) with periods of travel or residence in another district (the Northern area). The actual length of time spent in an area whose linguistic features differ from those of the principal domicile might be estimated from the number and frequency of occurrence of the deviant usages as well as from the extent to which such items remain confined to noncentral systems. Very lengthy residence outside the predominant area would never completely obliterate the traces of the original fundamental systems (phonology, closed portions of the morphology, and syntax), but it might produce some minor modifications.

3.6 Geoethnography

In the course of time, individuals, tribes, and nations change their location, and, as indicated in preceding sections, one may trace these migrations and travels via diverse linguistic techniques. The foregoing analyses have focused predominantly on reconstructing the history of individuals or groups wherever they went, as by tracing the Celtic place names across Europe to follow the migrations of the tribes. On the other hand, one may wish to reconstruct the demographic history of a particular terrain, identifying the different peoples who have passed that way, some to stay for only a short time, others for a longer period.

3.61 Toponymics: The Study of Place Names

A simple example will clarify one type of insight which toponymic (place-name) analysis can provide. The linguist can divide the phrase *Torpenhow Hill* (England) into its constituents, *tor, pen, how,* and *hill,* each traceable to a different linguistic source. The first element, *tor,* derives from Old English *torr,* a loan from Latin (which, in turn, acquired the morpheme from Greek at a much earlier period). One might reasonably assume that the *torr* element, then, dates from the period of Roman occupations of what was later to become England—an era prior to the withdrawal of the Romans in 410 or the invasions of the West Germanic tribes after 449. The Romans undoubtedly called the place *turris,* 'tower' or 'fortified height.' The Brythonic Celts, who later moved into the area after the Roman legions had departed, understood this *turris* or *torr* as the name of the hill, not as a description, since the word would have have little meaning to them. Consequently, they added their own word *penn,* 'hill,' making the name *torr penn,* to be understood as *Torr Hill.* Later, Scandinavian invaders took control of the area. On being informed that the name of the hill was *Torr Penn,* they added their own word for 'hill," namely *haugr,* not knowing that the earlier name already included at least one element, and perhaps two, having the same meaning. Eventually, with the warfare between the Scandinavians and the Old English, the latter group moved back into the area. In a fashion parallel to what had transpired before, on finding the name of the hill to be *Torrpenn Haugr,* they added their own word for 'hill'—whence emerges *Torrpenn-haugr Hill,* the ancestor of the modern form, meaning 'hill, hill, hill, hill.'

Although some of the details require additional analysis omitted here, this example does illustrate the persistence of toponyms and their possible use in demographic reconstruction. As seen, many toponymics reflect simple descriptive labeling, often reinforced for reasons similar to that of the successive layers of 'hill.' Thus the names *Avon, Esk, Usk,* and *Wye* simply preserve Celtic words for 'river' or 'water.' The Celtic *cumb* 'valley' appears in words such as *Duncombe* or *Winchcombe.* These and other names establish the fact of a Celtic substratum in England.

In some instances the internal details of form allow the analyst to assign dates to the period of entry of the word in question. For example, the Roman impact in the southern sections of Britain caused the Celtic tribes to adopt about six hundred Latin words, including *castra,* 'a fortified camp,' which was borrowed in turn by the Old English and added to many place names. Since the incorporation of the word antedated the sound change of *c* (phonological /k/) to *ch* (phonological /č/, still written *c* in Old English times but later respelled *ch*), the fact that *Winchester, Colchester, Portchester,* and other names employing the Latin-derived noun display the modern reflex of this *c-to-ch* mutation (namely the current pronunciation) suggests that the names were formed prior to the date of the change, or else such a word borrowed with a /k/ pronunciation would have retained that /k/. Sound changes allow no real exceptions. Apparent (but spurious) exceptions may abound, however, and simply require additional criteria for explanation. For instance, although most English words which used the *castra* element normally show *-chester* as the result of the change, some, such as *Lancaster* or *Dorcaster,* do not. One seeming explanation would be that the compounding in these words took place after the change had taken place, hence that these words never were affected by it. A glance at a chart showing the original distribution pattern of the /k/-to-/č/ shift reveals a northern boundary just south of the Humber River; hence words from the northern regions cannot be dated on the basis of this change (although they may be datable by other criteria). This differentiation appears in the Northern *kirk* which corresponds to the Southern *church.* There are other potential complications which need not be considered here; what is central is the fact that even without the well-attested documents pertaining to the history of England (or any other area), one can *(a)* readily identify earlier substrata and *(b)* even relegate these to their proper time depths (whether relative or absolute).

The distribution and number of place names may also allow an assessment of the extent of a foreign impact. For instance, well over 1400 Scandinavian place names still exist throughout England, but these are almost exclusively restricted to the area mapped as Scandinavian by the Treaty of Wedmore of 878. Furthermore, most of these appear in the counties of Lincolnshire and Yorkshire. Over six hundred names include -*by* (e.g., *Derby, Rugby, Whitby*), the Danish word for 'town' or 'farm' (cf. the word *by-law*—'town law'). Around three hundred names include the Scandinavian *thorp* 'village,' cognate with the Latin *turba* 'crowd,' as in *Bishopthorpe, Linthorpe*, or *Oglethorpe*. Another three hundred names include *thwaite* 'isolated land area,' as in *Applethwaite* or *Satterthwaite*. Of course, once an element has appeared often enough it may well become a productive formative of the language and thus enter into new combinations, but the extent and distribution of the names is indicative of the history of the area. Furthermore, these elements did not become productive, hence their value as clues.

3.62 Topidionymics: The Study of the Distribution of Personal Names

Another type of onomastic study, topidionymics, can reinforce or replace the simple toponymic information provided in the last section, at least within a limited range. For example, the medieval records of Yorkshire, Lincolnshire, Cumberland, Westmoreland, and Norfolk, precisely those areas with the greatest preponderance of Scandinavian toponyms, show a striking parallelism in the percentages of Scandinavian personal names. Thus one finds characteristic devices such as compounding with elements like -*son* to form *patronymics* ('names signifying one's parentage') of the type *Robinson, Johnson,* or *Stevenson*. Even if one lacked nonlinguistic evidence, the *idionyms* would attest the areas of Scandinavian impact, sometimes with, sometimes without the possibility of dating through knowledge of the special phonological or other details.

One may see how the invention of the telephone may well prove invaluable to the historian of the future since the telephone directory will serve as a repository for ethno- and demographic distribution in any specific area. Thus, for instance, a simple count of the number of Irish names listed in the New York City Directory tells what percentage of that city's population belong to this background.

Many names show their origin rather transparently (e.g., O'Neil, O'Bryan, etc.) However, one must exercise some caution so as to avoid being misled by occasional coincidences of form. For example, the prefix *Mac* is a typical Scoth patronymic, meaning 'son' or 'son of,' cognate with the *Mc* of Irish, the *map* of Welsh, and the *mai-* of English *maiden* (the Proto-Indo-European word may have meant 'offspring' rather than 'son' or 'male offspring'). Thus one gets *Macready, Macdougal,* and so on. Yet the name *Macris,* which also has a *Mac-* element, is often mistaken for Scotch although it actually comes from a Greek source unrelated to the *Mac-* forms of the Celtic. Such complications, of course, would not materially affect large-scale analytic results (i.e., how many irregular *Mac-* or other homophonic forms are likely to occur in a substantial name count?). As always, it is the totality of patterning that counts, not just the isolated detail.

A systematic study of idionymic (personal-name) distribution in different places may serve as a more reliable index of migration patterns than does the analysis of toponyms since statistically the number of place names must be considerably fewer than the number of names of the inhabitants of a place. Thus, for instance, the comparison of the former distribution of personal names in English with the names in colonial America has provided historians with a basis for identifying the particular areas of England from which migration to America took place. A further study of the idionyms is now leading to a reconstruction of the lines of settlement of the colonists. Such analyses may rest on parish registers, marriage, birth, or baptismal records, census lists, or, in the more modern period, on telephone directories.

3.7 Physical Topography

Toponymic analysis provides information not merely of the people who have once resided in an area, but also of the geographical features themselves—the lakes, the rivers, the streams, the mountains, sometimes even the types of vegetation, despite the fact that occasionally such features may have changed or disappeared. For example, today one finds forests of pine trees in Cuba limited mainly to a couple of regions—i.e., the Isle of Pines and the piedmont belt of part of Pinar del Rio Province, on the one hand, and the mountains (particularly the Nipe Mountains) of eastern Cuba, on the other. Yet pine trees once grew in many other regions of the island, a fact attested both by the dessicated pine cones that may easily be found on certain sites and also by the writings of observers of more than a century ago. Thus, for instance, in 1854 the geographer Pichardo referred to ten sabanas (plains covered by grasses, sedges, and low trees), nine of them "with pine trees and one without pines" in the area of San Juan y Martinez (see Note). The one-time presence of pines is still reflected linguistically by place names containing words such as *pino, pinar,* or *pinal: Sabana Pinal Alto, Pinar del Rio, Santa Cruz de los Pinos, Sabana de los Pinos,* or *Pinal de la Catilina.* Although most of the geographic literature on Cuba omits all reference to pines in Habana Province, a map of 1898 shows *El Pino* northeast of Guanaboa; *Los Pinos* south of the same place; *Pinar* in the vicinity of Arroyo Naranjo, *Pedro Pino,* near Sabanilla; not to mention *Pinos,* north of Managua; *Pinales* between Santiago de las Vegas and Managua; *Los Pinos* north of La Salud; *Pinar de Cazazon,* south of there; another *Los Pinos,* south of San Antonio de las Vegas; and a fourth *Los Pinos,* just southeast of Melena del Sur; as well as *Arroyo de los Pinos,* in the Sabana de Robles.

Details either not marked at all or not clearly marked on maps may be reconstructed by means of a proper understanding of the topographic nomenclature. Thus, to continue with the Cuban example, the labels *sabana, sabanilla* or *sabanita, sabanaza,* and *sabaneton* differentiate the actual size of grasslands on a descending, large-to-diminutive scale. Consequently, when a military map of

Cuba from 1898 discloses fifty-one names containing *sabana* (e.g., *Sabana la Mar, La Sabana Nueva, Las Sabanas de Minas, Sabana Traquera*), twenty-six containing *sabanilla* (e.g., *Sabanilla de Lara, Sabanilla de Otero, Sabanilla de Palma*), four with *sabanita* (*La Sabanita de Guyos* and three others plain *sabanita*), two with *sabanazo* (both of them just plain *Sabanazo*), and one with *sabaneton* (*Sabaneton de Satirio*), it is providing more information than just the names of places.

One finds typical varieties of vegetation associated with such toponymics as *ciego* (Spanish for 'blind'), *sao* ('patch of wood'—particularly one containing the palm trees yarey and cana and also the hardwood guayacan), and *cayo* (literally 'small island,' but the word is applied also to isolated and restricted areas of forest). Thus the same map referred to above lists thirty-one names with *ciego* (e.g., *Sabana del Ciego, Ciego Viamones, Ciego Caballo, Ciego de Avila, Ciego de Escobar*), seven with *sao* (e.g., *Sao de Palma, Sao Pepe,, Sao Limpio, Sao Arriba*), and six with *caya* (e.g., *Cayo Ingles, Cayo del Toro, Cayo Obregon*). An accurate interpretation of these place names, then, may serve as a guide to the vegetative make-up of the areas thus labeled.

Quite apart from the foregoing, one may note that sporadically similar kinds of information become fossilized in the communication system in different ways. For example, in the Ancient Egyptian hieroglyphic writing system, the symbol representing the Upper Kingdom (south Egypt, one part of the two kingdoms of the Nilotic civilization) was a stylized representation of the sedge, a flowering plant once found extensively in that area, though not in the Northern Kingdom. This kind of isolated information, though useful or interesting where noted, of course, must necessarily play a subordinate role in any systematic reconstructive analysis.

NOTES

Subsection 3.1

If one were to start from a position of absolutely no knowledge at all about possible genetic relationships among any two or more languages, the primary tools for the investigation would be dictionaries, glossaries, and grammars of the languages concerned. Then a word-by-word search would uncover similarities of lexicon and consistent phonological, morphological, or other correspondences. In fact, of course, much of the preliminary work has been done for most of the known languages. The best display of the proof of such genetic relationships, however, appears in the etymological dictionaries, which list the cognate forms. The majority of these dictionaries focus on a single language at a time but with some (usually unsystematic) display of related words in the kindred tongues descended from the same presumed source. In a few instances, notably for those language families such as the Indo-European which have been best studied, scholars have compiled dictionaries which give the reconstructed protoforms with nearly complete listings of attested forms descended from these. One such standard work is the *Vergleichendes Worterbuch der indogermanischen Sprachen,* edited by A. Walde and J. Pokorny.

Limited listings of selected vocabulary, particularly of languages not often studied, appear scattered through the regular issues of, or as supplements to, various learned journals. Often the purpose of such studies is the establishment of preliminary approximations to a family tree genealogy, with a view to suggesting degrees of closeness or distance of genetically related groups of languages. No complete listing of this type of work is possible here because of the number of languages concerned. Representative samplings, however, would be Joseph H. Greenberg, *The Languages of Africa* (Indiana University Research Center in Anthropology, Folklore and Linguistics, 1966); Sarah C. Gudschinsky, *Proto-Popotecan: A Comparative Study of Popolocan and Mixtecan* (I.U.R.C.A.F.L., 1959); G. Kingsley Noble, *Proto-Arawakan and Its Descendants* (I.U.R.C.A.F.L., 1965); and Robbins Burling, *Proto-Lolo-Burmese* (I.U.R.C.A.F.L., 1967).

One might note incidentally that with the passage of time occasional historical relationships only suspected before are being identified and worked out in detail. Thus, for example, Samuel E. Martin collected cognate forms and gave a statement in "Lexical Evidence Relating Korean to Japanese," in *Language,* 42 (1966), 185-251, and Roy Andrew Miller (*The Japanese Language*) promptly followed this insight by placing Japanese-Korean within the Altaic family. In a similar fashion the Chad family of languages was shown to belong to the Afro-Asiatic (also called Hamito-Semitic), and, later, another group of African languages was demonstrated to be a subdivision of Chad. The historian concerned with early phases of history must therefore keep himself informed about any such studies which relate to his own field of specialization.

Subsection 3.2

The primary goal of the analysis discussed in 3.2 is as nearly a complete reconstruction of the protolexicon as feasible. Consequently, the analyst may start, where possible, with dictionaries of the type which list already reconstructed protoforms with their deduced protomeanings (e.g., Walde and Pokorny, *Vergleichendes Worterbuch der indogermanischen Sprachen*). If no such reference works exist for the particular linguistic family that he is handling, he must do his own reconstruction by the use of any available dictionaries and grammars of those languages which have descended from the ancestral source. The researcher then would concentrate on identifying cognate vocabulary items, that is, those words with the appropriate phonological correspondences—or, in still other words, those which clearly demonstrate that they have undergone all of the sound changes from earliest times, hence that they must have been in the language from the protoperiod. The investigator must next group this reconstructed lexicon into related semantic headings —flora, fauna, and so on; then his task is one of identifying the primal home through the use of this evidence.

In rare instances the analyst may find that both the reconstruction and the semantic grouping have already been done, in whole or in part. For example, C. D. Buck has done such a study for Indo-European in his *Dictionary of Selected Synonyms in the Principal Indo-European Languages* (Chicago: University of Chicago Press, 1949). This particular work is not really complete since it omits many words that could have been reconstructed, and it also completely ignores much of the available evidence in a number of Indo-European languages. Nevertheless, as far as it does go (1515 pages, exclusive of the Preface), it is still highly useful. In a number of instances, individual studies of specific words have superseded Buck's reconstructions and explanations, but thus far no all-encompassing study has become available to replace his compendium. As already indicated, because of the great number of languages and language families, the individual investigator will have to determine for himself whether work-saving aids such as the foregoing volume exist for his own field of study or if he himself must do the reconstruction.

Fragmentary reconstructions of portions of the vocabulary of a number of genetically related families appear in a number of works whose main purpose is the establishment of these groups as language families. Thus in *The Languages of Africa* (Publication 25 of the Indiana University Research Center in Anthropology, Folklore, and Linguistics, 1963), Joseph H. Greenberg gives limited but useful word lists for Niger-Kordofanian (52 words), Nilo-Saharan (161 words), Khoisan (116 words), and Afro-Asiatic (78 words). Robbins Burling does much the same thing on a slightly larger scale (445 words) in his *Proto Lolo-Burmese* (Publication 43 of the Indiana University Research Center in Anthropology, Folklore, and Linguistics, 1967), which deals with six languages forming a subgroup of the Tibeto-Burmese family, itself a branch of Sino-Tibetan. Similar studies exist for a great many other language families, but obviously no systematic or extensive bibliography is possible here. It should be noted, however, that where the particular reconstructed lexicon happens by chance to contain critically demarcative words, the analyst can often identify the primal homeland even without a nearly complete listing of the vocabulary. Needless to say, the more extensive collections provide important corroborative evidence as well as additional insight, but the historian need not eschew the task of reconstruction simply because he does not have all of the tools he would like to have. Often even just a few words of the protolexicon can suffice to prove or disprove a hypothesis based on non-linguistic evidence.

Subsection 3.3

One may reconstruct the path of migration in a number of major ways. The analytic techniques would vary accordingly. One such approach would simply examine the place names on the map and identify their linguistic sources. Obviously the starting tools for this method would be the relevant maps themselves plus relevant etymological dictionaries of place names, where such exist. Further breakdown would depend on the investigator's ability to identify the languages from which the names come. Dictionaries and grammars would help here. Many geographical compilations also give glossaries of recurrent place descriptives such as *Nada* or *Naka,* the Japanese words for 'sea' or 'middle,' respectively; *By,* the Scandinavian (i.e., Danish, Norwegian, or Swedish) word for 'town'; or *Inish,* the Celtic word for 'island'; and so on. When the place name has undergone phonological change from the form it had at the time of first use, the appropriate historical grammar may allow a precise dating, whence identification of the time at which the naming took place. When the original namers no longer reside in the area, this dating indicates approximately when they passed through or resided in the area.

A second means of identifying migration patterns and ancient contacts is the systematic study of loan words, with a view to getting the sources and their dates. Here dictionaries are useful. Any etymological dictionary, supplemented by phonological grammars for the working out of relative chronologies, would suffice, however. The working principle of such an investigation is the assumption that for language A to have borrowed words from language B, the speakers of the two languages must have had some contact at the time of the transaction. A simple dating, then, of the period at which the words passed into the borrowing language establishes the time of the contact—with whatever geographical inferences may be drawn therefrom. A casual count of the number of words involved gives a glimpse of the extent of the impact, whether a few merchants or wanderers visited, in a transient way, or two whole nations resided side by side for prolonged interaction. A breakdown of the borrowed lexicon by semantic fields provides information on what kind of interaction took place.

Subsection 3.61

The starting point for toponymic analysis is any relevant map or chart with the names themselves. Some dictionaries of place names exist for specific areas, but unfortunately no one reference work as yet has appeared with a comprehensive listing for all place names. Some of the studies that do exist, however, give the etymologies of the toponyms. What is of major concern to the historian, of course, is the source language of the linguistic elements. In the absence of works dealing with the particular names under investigation, the analyst must resort to dictionaries and grammars.

Care must be employed to avoid misinterpretation of random and superficial similarities. If the speakers of a given language played any historic or prehistoric role in an area, normally more than one place name will preserve this influence. The dating of the place names can be done by the phonological changes which the words did or did not undergo. Sometimes where there is a clustering of place names from one source, the phonology of one of the words may fix an early date after which the word was first used and that of another word may give a later date before which the names entered. It is a reasonable though not necessarily certain assumption that in at least many instances the whole set of "foreign" names reflects the same period of historical influence. Where there are independent influences at different times, one may expect some of the place names to be assignable to each of the chronological periods. Here, as elsewhere, it must be emphasized, it is the patterning of the names, not the occurrence of a single name, which may be taken as convincing evidence. A single name of particular presumed provenience may alert one to look for additional evidence of the same kind, but is generally unreliable as an index by itself because it may well represent only a chance phonological resemblance to the foreign source-word in question.

Subsection 3.7

Leo Waibel, "Place Names as an Aid in the Reconstruction of the Original Vegetation of Cuba," *The Geographical Review*, XXXIII (1943), 376-396. What deserves particular attention here is the fact that, basing his analysis in large part on purely linguistic evidence, Waibel actually produced the first detailed vegetation map of Cuba. A special point worthy of note is Waibel's estimate of the specific area in square kilometers of each of the major topographic features—hardwood forest, pine forests, and so on—with his accurate approximations guided greatly by the nomenclature.

4. COMMUNICATIONAL SYSTEMS
IN PERSPECTIVE

All communicational systems, regardless of type, subdivide into two main parts: *(a)* the devices used to convey meanings or percepts, and *(b)* the meanings or percepts themselves. Much needless debate and misunderstanding has taken place because of the failure to grasp this fundamental dichotomy. Most linguists of recent decades have focused their attention on the devices, the manifesting marks of a system, rather than on either the meanings indigenous to the system or on the correlations between the manifesting marks and the meanings, except in the most trivial, differential way (e.g., Does this word have the same meaning as that one, or a different meaning, regardless of what that meaning is?). Simple systems, such as those employed by various species of animals (e.g., bees), permit only limited types of information to be conveyed (e.g., danger or the presence of food—here pollen—at a specific distance and in a given direction from the hive), while the more elaborate systems, such as the languages used by human beings, permit almost any type of information to be conveyed. The nature of the meanings, the types of devices used to signal those meanings (e.g., a type of dance pattern for the bees or the types of languages and gestural systems among humans), the hierarchal level, relative efficiency, and dynamics of the devices, and so on will form the basis for later discussion. The central point to be grasped here is the difference between the conceptual system (composed of its own subdivisions) and the various ways of signaling the meanings of that system.

4.1 Manifesting Systems

Manifesting systems take a variety of forms, all of which have one overriding prerequuisite: they must be perceptible to the intended audience, whether by sight, sound, touch, smell, or some other means. Thus the bee performs his figure-8 dance whose axis (the line which bisects both loops) signals the direction of the food source and whose timing (complete figures per unit time) signals the distance. The beaver slaps his tail on the water with a resounding whack to signal to other beavers the presence of immediate danger. The dog nuzzles his master and cuddles up to signal his affection. At other times he growls both to express his anger at intruders and to warn them off.

Human beings likewise employ a variety of manifesting outlets, such as speech (which relies on the perception of sound), writing (which relies on the perception of visible signals), gesture (which relies on the perception of a different type of visible signal), even touch (e.g., the tap on the shoulder during a dance to convey the information that one wishes to cut in), or smell (of only slight importance to humans, as in the use of perfumes, but of great importance to certain other species of animals).

The use of one manifesting outlet rather than another sometimes has strategic advantage, but central to the communicative act is the correlation between the manifesting signal and the meaning or meanings it signals. Sometimes one has a choice as to which signal to employ to convey the same message. For example, one may say the word *Stop!* (that is, produce the phonological set of signals represented by linguists as /stap/), spell out the letters of the visible analogue of the word, simply hold up one's hand in a convention-determined palm-outward gesture (as employed by a traffic policeman), or even convey the same message by a red light (as in the traffic signals common to many though not all countries). Contrary to popular belief, there is no inherent and necessary correlation between the signal and the meaning. The English speaker, for example, may signal 'yes' by an up-and-down nodding of his head and 'no' by a side-to-side gesture. The Albanian reverses the correlation, signaling 'no' by the nodding and 'yes' by the side-to-side gesture. Both the English and the Albanian speakers, of course, can also encode the message into either a phonological pattern (Albanian /po/ 'yes' or /yo/ 'no') or an orthographic pattern (i.e., spell out either *yes* or *no* or *po* or *yo*).

Obviously for either would-be communicator to employ the gestural code he must be certain *(a)* that his audience is looking at him and *(b)* that there is sufficient light for the audience to see the gesture. To take account of one possible pathological complication, the would-be communicator must also be certain *(c)* that his audience is not blind. If, for any of the foregoing reasons, the gesture were not perceivable by the audience, the communicator might switch to another manifesting outlet, such as the phonological. Thus, for example, if he spoke rather than gestured, even a blind person or, alternatively, a sighted person in a dark room would hear him and thus receive the message. Conversely, against a noise-filled background a gestural pattern might be preferable to a phonological one (at least for an audience which could see). Sometimes the particular choice of manifesting outlet would make little difference since any available signal would be received. The potential advantages of the phonological as opposed to the visual means of signaling—e.g., receivability both when the audience is facing away and when the light is insufficient—may help explain, however, why human beings have relied more heavily on the acoustic means of communication and have evolved more complex phonologically-based patterns in preference to, as well as in addition to, the other types of patterning.

As is evident, then, the code employed by human beings is convention-determined, and, therefore, another prerequisite of successful communication is often the audience's recognition not only of the details of the code but even of what code is being used. Consider, for instance a situation in which an Albanian girl signals 'no' by her standardized up-and-down gesture of the head to an English speaker who takes that same signal as 'yes.' The consequences could be disastrous, to say the least. This example is somewhat contrived, but less striking illustrations of the same type of misassignment abound in everyday life since all members of a macrosociocultural system belong to different subsets of that pattern, each with some differentiation from the others even where there is substantial overlap in both the percept systems and the manifesting systems. Take the nationally reported case of a white student at Wesleyan University who referred to a black classmate as a "punk." His intent was clearly to be insulting, but to the white student the word *punk* meant merely 'an undesirable person of little importance.' Unfortunately, in this instance, the meaning of the word in the black student's lexicon equated with 'homosexual,' hence the signal was more than merely an insult: it was a direct challenge to the classmate to prove his manhood. Consequently, the latter cornered the first student, who had not intended any such challenge, in the shower room and beat him up rather badly.

Manifesting systems subdivide into two major levels:

(1) Those portions which do not correlate *directly* with any meanings or percepts

(2) Those portions which do correlate with meanings. Ultimately, of course, it is the meanings or percepts themselves which are of central consequence to the social scientist, but an overview of the mechanisms for condensing, storing, and conveying the meanings is a necessity for grasping the means of analysis which lead to those insights.

4.11 Non-concept-correlated Building Blocks

Non-concept-correlated building blocks are those elements, such as the functional units of sound (the *phonemes*) or of writing (the *graphemes*—more conventionally called "letters") which signal no meanings by themselves in their capacity as phonemes or as graphemes. For example, what is the meaning of /b/ (the sound unit) or of *b* (the letter or grapheme)? The answer, of course, is that these units have no meaning in the usual sense, but they do occur in combinations with other phonemes or graphemes, and these combinations do correlate with meanings, as the /b/ in /bɪg/ which correlates in English with the meaning 'large.'

The only fundamental requirement of any phoneme *as a phoneme* is that it be different from every other phoneme in the same language. That is, unless /b/ and /p/ differ from one another in some identifiable way, the words *big* and *pig* of English would

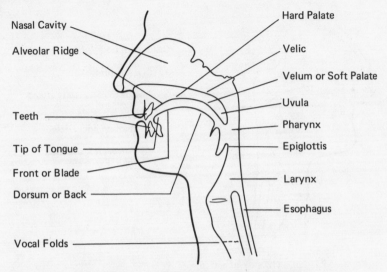

Nasal Cavity

Alveolar Ridge

Teeth

Tip of Tongue

Front or Blade

Dorsum or Back

Vocal Folds

Hard Palate

Velic

Velum or Soft Palate

Uvula

Pharynx

Epiglottis

Larynx

Esophagus

Fig. 2   THE ARTICULATORY TRACT (CROSS SECTION)

sound alike and thus be indistinguishable, as would *bat* and *pat, bin* and *pin,* and so on. These building blocks which are put together to form the meaningful signals do not themselves constitute the lowest level of language since every phoneme (or grapheme, etc.) consists of a combination of fundamental units or distinctive features. Thus in its totality the /b/ consists of *(a)* a complete closure of the lips, *(b)* the vibration of the vocal folds in the throat, and *(c)* a complete closure of the opening into the nasal cavity. (For a clarification of these articulatory manipulations, see Fig. 3.) If, on the other hand, the vocal folds were held tensely so that they did not vibrate, a /p/ would result. Alternatively, if the opening into the nasal cavity were not shut off, an /m/ would result. If the closure were made at some point other than the lips, some other phoneme —say /d/ or /g/—would result, and in each instance the resulting message would be different. Thus units having no meaning in themselves combine to form the more complex combinations of signals which do correlate with arbitrarily assigned meanings.

No language known possesses or needs more than thirty or forty minimal manifesting units such as phonemes. Many languages get along with far fewer. The potential sum of the combinations and permutations of these units is fantastically high. Furthermore, the phonemes and graphemes, or combinations of these that are cor-

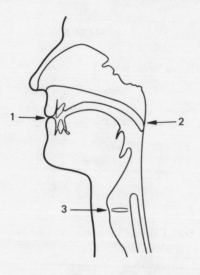

Features of both /p/ and /b/:

1. Lips compressed.

2. Passage to nasal cavity closed.

3. (a) For the /p/, the vocal folds do not vibrate.

   (b) For the /b/, the vocal folds do vibrate.

Fig. 3 ARTICULATION of /p/ and /b/

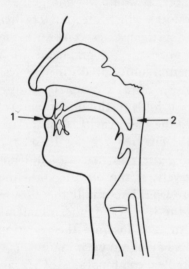

/m/

1. Lips compressed (as for /p/ or /b/).

2. Passage to nasal cavity open.

Fig. 4 ARTICULATION of /m/

related with meanings also combine in an increasingly complex hierarchy of signals so that no language lacks potential means for signaling everything its speakers can ever want to say. The underlying organizational pattern, however, is exceedingly simple. The phonemes (or graphemes) themselves rest on a smaller number of distinctive features, possibly no more than six to ten. No language utilizes all possible articulations. What is more, no language whatsoever uses exactly the same combination of distinctive features used by any other language.

What is of central importance for historians is the fact that the major principle of internal organization of any language is efficiency, although efficiency may be of various sorts, not all to be considered here. Each distinctive feature (vibrations of the vocal folds, for instance) enters into the production of many phonemes, not just one. Thus in English this voicing (vibration of the vocal folds) distinguishes an entire set of phonemes such as /b, d, g, v, z/ from another set, /p, t, k, f, s/ and so forth. Closure of the lips contrasts an entire set /b, p, m/ with other phonemes. Normally sound change takes place only in response to internal instability (to be defined below). When such change takes place, usually all phonemes which share a set of distinctive features being restructured or replaced *change as a set*. Thus, for instance, the group of sound changes formulated as Grimm's Law, and representing the initial stages of the phonological evolution from Indo-European to Germanic, consists of three interrelated *sets* of shifts:

1. All Indo-European phonemes sharing the features of both voicing and aspiration (the latter, a puff of air produced by the release of a closure) lost the feature of aspiration, whence b^h, d^h, g^h, and g^{hw} *became* b, d, g, and g^w, respectively in Germanic.

2. All Indo-European phonemes sharing the features of voicing and lack of aspiration lost the feature of voicing, whence *(b)*, d, g, and g^w became *(p)*, t, and k^w respectively in Germanic. (There is some question about whether Indo-European had a b, hence the parentheses around the b and p. Some scholars believe that the b in the few attested examples of cognate words with this phoneme arose secondarily from clusters of other consonants.)

3. All Indo-European phonemes sharing the features of voicelessness, nonaspiration, and complete closure lost the feature of complete closure, whence Indo-European p, t, k, and k^w became f, θ, χ *and* χ^w respectively in Germanic.

Grimm's Law, of greater interest to linguists than to nonlinguists, is given here mainly to illustrate the structural principle

operative in systemic dynamics. Grimm himself, who formulated
his statement in 1822, never quite grasped the cause of the sets of
changes. Had he done so, he would have realized that the developments were motivated by a structural instability—one which affected
all of the Indo-European languages. Furthermore, there were other
possible directions in which change could have taken place as a
result of the same instability. Germanic evolved in only one out of
the many possible directions. Other Indo-European languages
evolved differently, but all of the different changes were motivated
by the same underlying cause. The particular developments in one
or another language resulted directly from statistical factors which
gave greater value to one solution or another.

Furthermore, all of the developments in each Indo-European
language were actually predictable, given the relevant information
necessary to solve some rather complex equations. The situation
was not dissimilar to that of mathematical problems with various
possible solutions, all perfectly valid. What is most striking about
the entire complex of Indo-European developments, however, is
the fact that every possibility which could have taken place did take
place in some Indo-European branch. To illustrate this fact, one
must reconsider the entire set of Indo-European stops (those phonemes with a complete closure of the articulating organs).

This chart depicts *all* potential combinations of the distinctive
features or parameters of the stop system. Superimposed on the basic
chart is the particular set of phonemes incorporating those articulatory features, which is reconstructed for the parent Indo-European
language. from the evidence of the descendent dialects. As can be
seen, not all potential combinations of features actually did occur.
One may reconstruct, for instance, the feature of voicelessness because it appeared throughout the set p, t, k, and k^w, and contrasted
that set with another set—(b), d, g, and g^w, all of whose members
were voiced. One may also reconstruct the features of aspiration
or its lack because of the presence of b^h, d^h, g^h, and g^h , which contrasted with (b), d, g, and g^w respectively only by this one feature.
The projection of the potential combination of voicelessness and
lack of aspiration (depicted by empty boxes on the chart) results
from the working out of all attested features in all possible combinations. The presence of pairs such as the k which contrasts with
k^w or of the g which contrasts with g^w permits the projection of other

THE INDO-EUROPEAN STOPS AND THEIR DISTINCTIVE FEATURES

	LABIAL, NO CONCOMITANT LABIALITY	LABIAL, CONCOMITANT LABIALITY	APICAL, NO CON-COMITANT LABIALITY	APICAL, CONCOMITANT LABIALITY	DORSAL, NO CONCOMITANT LABIALITY	DORSAL, CONCOMITANT LABIALITY
VOICELESS UNASPIRATED	p		t		k	k^w
VOICED UNASPIRATED	(b)		d		g	g^w
VOICELESS ASPIRATED						
VOICED ASPIRATED	b^h		d^h		g^h	g^{hw}

Fig. 5

simplex units with potential colabialized correlates (i.e., t^w to t, d^w to d, etc.).

Why a system with holes in the pattern (i.e., unrealized intersections of distinctive features of the system) is unstable may become clearer from a consideration of part of the foregoing, namely just the phonemes at a single point of aperture (here that behind or against the upper-front teeth):

APICAL STOPS

	VOICED	VOICELESS
UNASPIRATED	/d/	/t/
ASPIRATED	/dʰ/	

Fig. 6

As seen from Figure 6 (the apical stops), the /d/ phoneme of Indo-European could not be aspirated or else it would have sounded like the /dʰ/, a different phoneme of the same system, and thus many words would have been pronounced alike. Likewise the same /d/ could not simply lose its voicing or else it would have sounded like the /t/ There was no short-range reason, however, why in any given instance the /t/ phoneme could not be produced with aspiration, that is as [tʰ], since there was no contrastive /tʰ/ in the system to cause confusion. Likewise there was no short-range reason why the /dʰ/ could not on occasion be produced as voiceless, that is, as [tʰ]. Yet, as illustrated by Figure 7 below (really Figure 6 revised to indicate the overlap at the intersection of "VOICELESS" and "ASPIRATED"), any /tʰ/ produced in this way as a nondistinctive variant (called an *allophone*, from *allo-* 'other' plus *phone* 'sound') of either /t/ or /dʰ/ could not readily be assigned by the audience, with absolute certainty, to the source phoneme, that is, to /dʰ/ not to /t/, or the reverse. Hence there would have been a long-range feedback.

	VOICED	VOICELESS
UNASPIRATED	/d/	/t/
ASPIRATED	/dʰ/	[tʰ]

Fig. 7

61078

When the /d/ phoneme transgressed its boundaries in the direction of /t/, there was a regular and *immediate* feedback: the audience always either misinterpreted or else failed to interpret the signal at all (much as might happen if a speaker of modern English should say *ten* instead of *den*). Thus the speaker immediately corrected himself. In the type of boundary violation involving overlap (technically called *bilateral allophony*), sometimes the audience did understand, but occasionally it did not. Yet even some misinterpretation causes eventual correction, but the Indo-European correction came by way of reordering of the phonological boundaries, a fundamental change in the structure of the system—a reshaping that gave rise to the different languages descended from Indo-European.

It is not the intent here to go into the details of how systems restructure or why the direction of the restructuring can often be predicted by analysts who understand the dynamics of systems, but, briefly, the unrealized intersections of parameters, constituting an instability, may be eliminated additively (e.g., by filling them, as Sanskrit did) or subtractively (e.g., by eliminating one or more of the intersecting parameters, as happened in Anatolian or Celtic). Sometimes when the mergers that would have ensued from the subtractive solution threatened important communicative distinctions, an initial impetus to a subtractive maneuver initiated an entire chain reaction, as seen in Germanic (Grimm's Law; also as seen in Armenian). The reason that one solution is acceptable to one genetically related system and unacceptable to another lies in the different developments of the two once they have diverged: certain words drop out, given different environmental conditions of the members of the sociocultural system; other words are added; still others appear with greater or less frequency. The statistical incidence of each phoneme and of the distinctive features that make up each phoneme then would differ, whence a difference in the systemic pressures. Still other possibilities existed as well, but for additional details the reader interested in pursuing the matter is referred to *Parametric Linguistics* and to *Multilateral Allovariance* (see Notes).

Given the structured nature of linguistic change then (illustrated here by the phonological-level developments of Grimm's Law, but operative in other modes and at other levels as well), one can readily see why scholars postulating a genetical relationship between two languages may consider fragmentary evidence important if it supports a parametric correlation already evident from other data. Thus, for instance, if there were many examples of Germanic f (and remember that English is a Germanic-derived language) corresponding to Latin or Greek p—e.g., *father, pater, pater; fish, piscis,* etc.— and some examples of Germanic θ (English *th*) corresponding to Latin or Greek t—e.g., English *thin,* Latin *tenuis*—even a single example or two of Germanic χ (later English h) correlating with Latin or Greek k—e.g., English *hundred,* Latin *centum,* Greek *(hé)-katon*—would match the assumed development of stop articulation (complete closure) switching to fricative articulation (incomplete closure) evident in the rest of the pattern. In fact such evidence would mean more to the linguist than a few more instances of the f-to-p or θ-to-t types.

The search for regularity of patterning as a basis for making certain inferences (e.g., genetic versus nongenetic relationships) rests on the observation that linguistic changes admit of no exceptions whatsoever. They have the force of a physical principle or law. Sometimes, however, apparent exceptions do exist, but this fact usually indicates either that the original "law" or principle has not been stated precisely enough or that later, secondary, developments have taken place. For instance, two major classes of "exceptions" to the Grimm's Law developments occur:

(1) The Indo-European phonemes $p, t, k,$ and k^w did not shift to the anticipated Grimm's Law forms when they were preceded by s, as in the *st-* of the word for 'stand.' Thus the **st-* of the Indo-European form of the word remained *st-* in the evolution to Germanic, whence English, as in modern English *stand,* just as the same **st-* cluster remained in Latin, attested by *stāre.*

(2) The Indo-European phonemes $p, t, k,$ and k^w, having undergone the Grimm's Law shift to fricatives, underwent a second set of changes in certain environments relating to voicing and the original position of the Indo-European accent. (This was first formulated by Karl Verner in 1875, and is therefore referred to as Verner's Law.) The details are irrelevant here. What is relevant, however, is the fact that the apparent exceptions themselves fit a pattern, and, once

one knows this pattern, a more sharply defined statement predicts the correlations.

4.12 Concept-correlated Building Blocks

As has been suggested, the phonemes, graphemes, or other manifesting signals of various types do not—in their capacity as phonemes, graphemes, etc.—correlate with any meanings. However they do combine to form higher-level units which function as meaning-bearers. Thus the phonemes /p/ and /ɪ/ and /n/ carry no meaning by themselves, but when they appear together in relevant ways, they do have meanings arbitrarily associated with each amalgam. When juxtaposed in one order (e.g., /pɪn/), they may correlate with one meaning or set of meanings ('pin'); when juxtaposed in another order (e.g., /nɪp/), they may correlate with another meaning or set of meanings ('nip'). Not all potential combinations of the conceptually uncorrelated building blocks have meanings assigned to them. Thus, in English, the combination /pnɪ/ would be meaningless. The smallest meaningful combinations of otherwise meaningless manifesting units (the phonemes, graphemes, etc.) are called *morphemes*. As seen, these meaning-bearers consist of certain perceptible units of form and of the relative sequence of these forms: a change of position would either change the meaning correlated with the group or would render the group meaningless.

This combination of form and position (or relative sequence) repeats in a continuous hierarchy of manifesting-level building blocks. Morphemes combine to make higher-level signals such as words. Thus *man* and *-hood* make *manhood,* combining the meanings of *man,* 'human, male,' and of *-hood,* 'state of being.' Here too, however, the position as well as the form is important. One could not, for example, shift the position of the morphemes to *hoodman* without destroying or changing the meaning to be correlated with the complex. Words in turn may combine in a fixed sequence to make phrases—e.g., *to the man*—and a shift of sequence *(man the to)* may destroy the message of the combination as such, or else change it. Thus relative position itself often serves as a meaningful signal. Phrases in turn combine to make higher-level phrases, and so on, up to the highest levels in the communicative hierarchy. At each stage the relative position of a functional unit with respect to other functional units is important. The sequences *The man saw the woman* and *The woman saw the man* do not signal the same message since the preverbal position of one noun phrase marks it as the subject, and the postverbal position of the other noun phrase marks it as the object.

There is nothing at all, however, which requires that any given function (for example, here the subject-marking or the object-marking function) must be signaled at one level in the hierarchy rather than at another. Latin, for instance, marked the same subject- and object-functions by morphological endings attached to nouns or adjectives and, thus, did not rely upon the order of the words for this purpose. For instance, in Latin *Vir fēminam vīdit* and *Fēminam vir vīdit* and *Vīdit fēminam vir* and *Vīdit vir fēminam,* as well as other possible sequences, all signaled the same message, 'The man saw the woman.' The *-m* of *fēminam* marked the word as the object rather than the subject. Latin reflected the earlier Indo-European way of marking this function. Since English, too, descends from the Proto-Indo-European language, one may surmise that when certain phonological changes caused the original object-marking *-m* to disappear in the evolution of Indo-European to English, the language simply switched from a lower-level to a higher-level in the hierarchy, i.e., from morpheme choice to word order, to signal the same function. When this shift took place, the word order, which had previously been free, became fixed since it took on the burden of marking the meaning or function.

Not all languages distinguish a level in the concept-signaling hierarchy which can be called the "word," as English and other Indo-European languages do. However, traditionally those languages that do have words as distinct from morphemes or combinations of morphemes distinguish syntax and morphology as hierarchal levels. By this view, meaningful combinations up to the word level are designated as "morphology." Combinations above the word level are grouped together under the label "syntax." The principles governing the combinations of meaning-bearers of both these levels (where distinguished) are the same. Each functional form may have its own meaning and the relevant position of the functional units with respect to each other may signal other meanings.

Usually the total meaning of the utterance is the sum of the cumulative meanings signaled throughout the entire hierarchy. Sometimes, however, a combination of signaling units may also correlate as a larger unit with some meaning or set of meanings which is different from that of the cumulative meanings of the constituents. Such higher-level amalgams are *idioms*. For instance, the utterances *He kicked the ball, He kicked the chair,* and *He kicked the man* all signal the same message—one involving a particular kind of physical act performed with the feet. They differ only in the meanings of the object-nouns *ball, chair,* and *man.* On the other hand, the utterance *He kicked the bucket* correlates *as a total unit* with a set of conceptualizations 'He perished' unrelated to the meaning of *He kicked the* plus any unit other than *bucket.* The hierarchal level of the idiom given here is the sentential, but the same principle— namely, that some signaling units correlate with a given meaning or set of meanings only when in specific contexts but with some other meaning or set of meanings when not in that context—is operative at other levels. For example the word *go* starts out with the phonomes /g/ and /o/. Any time an English speaker hears these phonemes, he starts to correlate them with a conceptualization dealing with 'motion.' If, however, the phoneme /t/ were to follow the preceding two, giving /got/, he would abort the earlier decoding attempt and recorrelate the unit with 'goat.' In a special sense, then, /got/ is an idiom since the /go/, which may correlate with motion, enters into a different conceptual-correlation when this /t/ is present.

The areas of *morphology* and *syntax* group together to make the *grammar,* a modern view—not too well articulated—asserting in essence that grammar is that area of linguistics which deals with signal-units which correlate with meanings. As seen, sometimes the same meanings may be signaled at different hierarchal levels. Furthermore there are different manifesting modes for signaling meaning. The two discussed briefly above were phonology and graphology (writing systems). One may of course use other devices as signals, for example, flags or lanterns ("one if by land, two if by sea") and so on. Not all of these are relevant to historical studies. However, a later section will take up the problem of gesture systems, since they allow some historical reconstruction which can be significant.

4.2 Cognitive Systems

No member of a socioculture system, unless highly sophisticated because of professional interest and training, ever becomes consciously aware of all of the norms, culture-bound values, implicit assumptions, or perceptive distinctions which are held by himself and other members of his system and which govern his every action. He lives by this internalized pattern but is as incapable of analyzing or explaining it as he is of analyzing or explaining the way in which he digests his meals, a task more properly delegated to physiologists, nutritionists, chemists, or other specialists qualified to do the job. Yet all of the relevant features of his own sociocultural system as well as vestiges of the earlier systems out of which that one emerged are somehow crystalized and reflected in the communicational system which he employs in his daily life, both for actual communication (e.g., speaking, writing, and gesturing) and for thinking as well.

The manifesting devices described in preceding sections of this book constitute the perceptible portions of the communicational system, but their very existence presupposes something which lies behind the visible details: if they signal or make something manifest, what is it which they signal? The answer to that question is a total description of the entire sociocultural system. The members of the system perceive, think, and communicate those elements which are relevant to that particular society. They ignore or are unaware of that which is irrelevant to them; they observe, and eventually encode, all that is relevant to them—and only that which is relevant. An inventory of the percepts lying behind the manifesting devices constitutes a sociocultural inventory. Section 5 will deal in detail with the analysis of sociocultural systems and will indicate how certain types of secondary sociocultural analysis by means of primary communicational analysis can disclose information of interest and importance to historians as well as to sociologists, anthropologists, psychologists, and other social scientists. Yet the following brief remarks, to be amplified and illustrated in the next section, may provide some perspective.

As we have seen, the same percept may be signaled either at different hierarchal levels (e.g., by bound morphemes or by the relative positions of words) or by different manifesting modes (phonological, gestural, etc.). Furthermore, many of the discrete "thoughts" regarded by those who chance to consider the matter as unitary are often themselves complex amalgams of smaller perceptual distinctions, analogous in a sense at the conceptual level to the phoneme at the manifesting level—the latter, in its turn, constituting a "bundle" of relevant articulatory features. In just such a way, some "thoughts," even of the simplest type, embody discrete differences and demarcative boundaries ascertainable only by appropriate contrastive analysis. Just as the range of articulatory positions open to a given phoneme in a system is determined by the existence—or nonexistence—of specific other phonemes in that system, so the range of meanings, say, of a color term may be determined by the number and range of meanings of other color terms in that same system.

Although the same or analogous percepts may be embodied in two different systems, the degree of incidence of those percepts may differ from system to system. This statistical measure would reflect the relative degree of importance of the underlying concepts. Furthermore, the percepts could be encoded into either obligatory or optional portions of the manifesting patterns of one or the other system. This difference also would reflect sociocultural differences.

The facts of the real world do not change, regardless of how men view that world. There were bacteria in the Middle Ages, and these same bacteria caused diseases then as they do now. Nevertheless, the different ways of observing the same facts (e.g., sickness as punishment for one's sins versus sickness as a result of bacteria-caused disruption of one's normal physiological processes) appear in the different communicational systems of the respective chronological periods. The communicational system then does reflect the real world, but only as filtered through the views (or technology) of the members of the perceiving sociocultural system. Real and perceptible differences in the environments of separate sociocultural systems do show up in the correlated communicational systems, as in the many words for 'snow' in one language but none in another which is spoken in a tropical region.

In the absence of mental telepathy or divine intuition, this percept inventory of each sociocultural system can only be carried out by the analysis of observable facts. Such an analysis may take many forms, one of which is that of applying appropriate procedures to the manifesting devices of communicational systems, since the manifesting devices are the only directly observable portions of the structures. In a similar way, the physicist observes the distinctive combinations of elements that actually do take place and which are accessible to direct observation, but he goes beyond the directly observable facts to construct a periodic table and to postulate certain assumptions about atomic structure. Although in certain superficial ways the methodologies differ, the communicational analyst proceeds—or may proceed—from the observed and verifiable manifesting devices to an analytic reconstruction of the cognitive system of its users, and from there to other inferences of historical and other interest.

NOTES

Most general introductory linguistic textbooks will prove helpful in achieving the perspective necessary to a sound analytic technique. No modern text covers all of the major areas of the field, but the following are useful.

Block, Bernard, and George L. Trager. *Outline of Linguistic Analysis*. Baltimore: The Linguistic Society of America, 1942.

Bloomfield, Leonard. *Language*. New York: Henry Holt and Co., 1933.

Bolinger, Dwight. *Aspects of Language*. New York: Harcourt, Brace & World, Inc., 1968.

Dinneen, Francis P. *An Introduction to General Linguistics*. New York: Holt, Rinehart and Winston, Inc., 1967.

Gleason, Henry A., Jr. *An Introduction to Descriptive Linguistics*, rev. ed. New York: Holt, Rinehart and Winston, Inc., 1961.

Hall, Robert A., Jr. *Introductory Linguistics*. Philadelphia: Chilton Books, 1964.

Hockett, Charles F. *A Course in Modern Linguistics*. New York: The Macmillan Co., 1958.

Hughes, John P. *The Science of Language: An Introduction to Linguistics.* New York: Random House, Inc., 1962.

Lyons, John. *Introduction to Theoretical Linguistics.* New York: Cambridge University Press, 1969.

Martinet, André. *Elements of General Linguistics,* trans. by Elisabeth Palmer, foreword by L. R. Palmer. Chicago: University of Chicago Press; London: Faber and Faber Ltd., 1964.

A useful, but more advanced study, which presupposes a thorough mastery of elementary theory, is the following:

Hoenigswald, Henry M. *Language Change and Linguistic Reconstruction.* Chicago: University of Chicago Press, 1961.

Advanced students may also find the following two works helpful in elucidating some of the structural dynamics and principles of systemic change:

Heller, L. G., and James Macris. *Parametric Linguistics.* Paris and The Hague: Mouton, 1967.

———. *Multilateral Allovariance.* London: The International Linguistic Association, 1972.

5. SOCIOCULTURAL RECONSTRUCTION

Section 1 of this book started with the assertion that "language eventually encodes . . . the relevant features of the sociocultural system of its speakers." As already seen in Sections 2 and 3, one can readily uncover important information regarding time and place by applying appropriate analytic techniques to communicational systems. The chronological and geographical insights reflect just part of the general range of knowledge open to the trained investigator. Systematic techniques allow a structural analysis of the entire cognitive scheme of the system as well as of the individual's place within the system. Section 6 will return to the latter (monanthropical) type of procedure. This section will deal with the broader picture.

Individual linguists and individual historians of an antiquarian, anecdotal turn of mind are fond of citing isolated etymologies which reveal this or that bit of particular insight into the history of the speakers of a language, e.g., analysis reveals that the word for 'in-laws' in one American Indian language means 'the ones for whom I carry packages.' Such analyses, which usually rest on constituent-structure segmentation, sometimes reinforced by comparative studies, can be charming and sometimes even meaningful if one has hit upon some critical fact, but they represent, often enough, accidental discoveries, most frequently found in the course of investigations directed toward some other end. Although the serious scholar can rejoice at such unlooked-for bonuses, he must not rest his investigative potentialities on sheer chance. He must have a reliable, consistent, and—above all—systematic technique for arriving at his insights. It is this kind of procedure which is the focus for the following remarks.

An analysis of all of the concept-correlated manifesting marks of a communicational system would, if aimed at the identification of the concepts behind the signals, lead to an inventory of distinctive percepts and of the statistical incidence of those percepts in the cognitive scheme of the members of the system. It would be a type of sociocultural index of what the people of the system view as relevant in their world. To be sure one would still find vestigial relics of 'the-ones-for-whom-I-carry-packages' sort, but one would also have the total inventory of the critical distinctions characteristic of the system at a given time. These percepts, one must recall, reflect a specific system, not every system. As seen in Section 3, the people in a subzero climate do not normally discuss or even think about bananas or coconuts if these items lie outside their range of experience. Thus they would have perhaps many different manifesting signals for 'snow' and 'ice' but none for the tropical fruits. Conversely a culture that relies heavily on bananas for subsistence would have many signals for all the percepts which are critical to a banana culture, but perhaps few or none for features of cold climates. The particular manner or level of the manifesting signal would be less relevant than the perceptual scheme itself. What is it which is being signaled? One would, of course, have to investigate all of the manifesting modes and all of the levels of each in the course of such a thorough analysis. For example, a word may signal one or more percepts, the position of the word with respect to other words in a phrase may signal other percepts, and the position of the phrase itself may relate to still other cognitions. Furthermore, even the gestural system with its structural components correlates with meanings. The prime target of this kind of investigation, however carried out and at whatever level, would be the cognitive scheme behind the manifesting plan since it is this cognitive scheme which reflects the sociocultural system itself.

Depending on one's purpose, one may investigate:

(1) A single sociocultural system at a single point in time

(2) Two or more sociocultural systems at the same point in time

(3) The history of a single sociocultural system, in essence a comparison of two or more systems at different points in time but connected by a continuous genetic relationship

(4) Two or more sociocultural systems of no genetic relationship at different points in time

If the two or more systems investigated under (2) should be genetically related, an appropriate investigation can lead to the reconstruction of (5) the prehistoric ancestor of the attested systems. Furthermore,
a similar prehistoric reconstruction can be carried out even if the
two or more compared systems are not synchronic provided only
that *(a)* they are genetically related and *(b)* they represent different
branches of the source system. The reconstruction of such a protosystem leads directly back to (3), the history of a single sociocultural
system, since this protosystem which represents an earlier phase of
each of the descendant systems may rightly serve as the starting point
for the comparison of two sequentially related patterns—a history.
Thus, even strictly synchronic evidence can provide the basis for
diachronic perspective.

The kinds of insight derivable from such sociocultural-percept
comparison transcend the purely historical, of course. This type of
diagnosis provides a true *comparability index*. Indeed, if the systems
are synchronic, it can provide a *compatibility index*, one which may
serve to predict the possible interactions between members of the
two systems. More will be said about this point later.

5.1 Monochronic, Monosystemic Analysis

As has been indicated, the starting point for various types of
sociocultural analysis and reconstruction is the mapping of a single
system. Even at the risk of undue repetition, it may be desirable to
restate the fundamental premises on which the analysis rests.

(1) The members of a sociocultural system think about those
elements of their system which are distinctive and relevant to them.
A converse of this statement, namely, that they do not think about
that which is irrelevant to them, should be, but is not always,
obvious.

(2) Human beings eventually incorporate the relevant features
of their cognitive system—itself the reflex of what is relevant to
their experience—into a communicational code.

(3) This encoding may be, and often, is redundant.

(4) This encoding may take any available manifesting outlet:
auditory, visual, and so on.

(5) It may utilize any of various hierarchal levels of a given manifesting outlet.

(6) The "items" of a manifesting outlet may symbolize more than one cognition at a time.

(7) A communicational system or set of systems serves not only communicational functions (this use is obvious) but also, of greater consequence, cognitional functions: it is a tool for crystalizing thought; without it higher and more complex cognition would be severely restricted.

(8) The analysis of a sociocultural system by means of its communicational system starts with the manifesting marks available for the investigation, but it *aims at an assignment of the marks* (whatever their form) *to cognitional percepts which lie behind the signals*. In other words, if there is a signal, precisely what does it signal?

(9) Since these percepts reflect the actual structure of the sociocultural system, an analysis of the cognitional scheme into which they enter is tantamount to an analysis of the macrosystem itself, or at the very least reflects such a system in some critical way.

Returning to the main purpose of this section then, how does one arrive at the percepts which correlate with the signals? Keeping in mind point (6) above—that the "items" of a manifesting outlet may symbolize more than one cognition at a time, consider the following set of English words (really only a representative sampling, not a full set):

boy	*girl*
man	*woman*
father	*mother*
uncle	*aunt*
nephew	*niece*
actor	*actress*

Obviously this particular list could be greatly enlarged, but one can readily see how important the male/female dichotomy is in the English system. This dichotomy presumably should exist in other cultures, whence have come the corresponding communicational systems, but the relative importance can only be measured by considering how well integrated into the system the conceptualization is. In the Afro-Asiatic group of languages, for example, verbs as well as nouns mark the male-versus-female contrast. One notes that in this latter group the roles of men and women are more markedly different than those seen for Indo-European-derived cultures.

One could arrange the items differently to bring out other important cultural contrasts, as in the following:

man	*boy*
woman	*girl*
horse	*colt*
dog	*puppy*
cat	*kitten*
lion	*cub*
cow	*calf*

Again, one sees that the criterion of age—i.e., older versus younger —plays a central role in our culture. Other dichotomous listings would bring out other cultural features. Some of these are found in other cultures, but still others are not. For example, English and other Indo-European-derived languages note differences such as the following:

father	*uncle*
mother	*aunt*
son	*nephew*
daughter	*niece*

This pattern represents direct versus collateral relationship. Yet many languages ignore the dichotomous grouping given here, lumping *father* and *uncle, mother* and *aunt, son* and *nephew,* and *daughter* and *niece* together under a single term for what appears in English as a set. The presence or absence of the contrast in the language reflects an organizational grouping embedded in the cultural system itself. For instance, in Pawnee, which uses the same word for *wife* and *sister* (of the wife), the husband has marital rights to the wife's sister as well as to the particular woman he marries.

Likewise, his brothers (the Pawnee word for husband and husband's brother is the name) have the same marital rights to the wife or her sisters. In this culture, there can be no concept such as 'cousin,' since the paternity of the offspring of such a union may not even be known. Thus an individual in this culture must regard the off-spring of a set of males and a set of females as either brothers or sisters. The term for what we would call uncle's wife (on the paternal side) is the same as that for wife—hence it should come as no surprise that in this culture a boy's first sexual encounter is regularly with his father's brother's wife (indiscriminately *aunt* to us but not to the Pawnee).

A communicational system must reflect the cultural scheme, or it is inadequate. The Lardil tribes of Australia, for instance, organize much of their activity around a complex, alternate-generation scheme. The Lardil will eat with, hunt with, and mate with those individuals who belong either to his own generation (as measured by the culture's own seemingly complex set of rules) or to any generation which is odd-numbered with respect to his own as the prime, but not with individuals of an even-numbered generation. This feature is embedded in the morphology and lexicon of Lardil, and its presence as a sociocultural percept would be disclosed by an analytic procedure similar to the one just given for the English lexicon. Yet, to illustrate points (3) and (5) of the premises of our technique, namely that communicative coding is often redundant (3) and that it may utilize any of various levels of the manifesting outlet(s), in Lardil, words belonging to odd- and to even-numbered generations cannot appear together in the same phase-structure. The fact that generational scheme plays an important role in the communicational system, i.e., *(a)* that it is incorporated into many morphemes and words, and *(b)* that it is incorporated into different levels—morphology, lexicon, and syntax, reflects the state of affairs of the Lardil macrosystem itself, in which all (to them) important activities are regulated by this set of percepts. Thus a Lardil man may not even converse directly with an individual from an incompatible generation. When a family sits down to a meal, the individuals group and position themselves in such a fashion that incompatibles don't even face one another.

Consider premise (4), that encoding may take any available

manifesting outlet. In Colombia, Spanish speakers utilize a gestural system which differentiates the signal for the height of an animal from that which marks the height of a human being, the palm being held horizontally for the former but vertically for the latter. The identical percept appears, likewise, in the phonic manifesting system, which has separate words for analogous parts of the bodies of animals and of human beings (e.g., *pata* 'foot of an animal' versus *pie* 'foot of a human being'). The fact that the same percept is encoded into more manifesting modes than one (i.e., into both the gestural and the phonic) serves as a diagnostic cue to the relative importance of the distinction to the sociocultural system, an insight confirmed by the presence of other words in the lexicon which signal the same contrast.

English, a language distinctly related to Spanish, also has some words which embed the contrast (e.g., *hoof* versus *foot*) but not as many as Spanish. Nor does English encode the distinction into its gestural system. This relative weight in importance of the human/nonhuman dichotomy reflects in some fashion the noncommunicational parts of the Spanish and English sociocultural systems. Thus, as has been suggested by some trained investigators, the attitudes of members of each system differ with respect to the treatment of animals. The Spanish-speaking man enjoys bull fighting, an activity outlawed in most of the English-speaking world. The difference in attitude rests on whether the bull is regarded as more similar or less similar to the human being, whence follows a difference in the classification of the baiting and killing of the bull either as sport or as cruelty. The same relative weight in importance of the percept to each of the systems appears in the presence of many organizations, such as the Association for the Prevention of Cruelty to Animals, in English-speaking countries.

The question arises (*a*) whether the communicational system conditions the thought processes and attitudes of its users, (*b*) whether it merely restructures to mirror those processes and attitudes, or (*c*) whether there is a reciprocal relationship, one in which the language modifies to reflect the noncommunicational patterning but then itself conditions the users to a distinctive world view which may change in the course of time, whence there will come additional changes in the communicational structures. The question is an important one from certain points of view, but the answer, which has occasioned much heated debate among linguists, and the basis for that answer would require a very substantial digression from the major intent of this book. This author holds that the reciprocal explanation best fits the known facts, but the particular choice of explanation does not significantly change the central point regarding the validity of an analysis of the communicational system as a means of arriving at a picture of the rest of the sociocultural structure.

The interpretation of manifesting-mark evidence requires some special consideration beyond those points already mentioned. Most though not necessarily all manifesting devices signal more than one percept at a time. Thus the word *man* represents simultaneously 'male' as opposed to 'female' (seen in the contrasting word *woman*), 'adult' as opposed to 'nonadult' (seen in the contrasting word *boy*), 'human' as opposed to 'nonhuman' (seen in the contrasting word *animal*), and so on.

Some manifesting marks, however, signal different meanings on an either/or basis as does the English word *punch* which may mean either 'a blow' or 'a type of drink.' Such examples pose a problem of analysis. Do the different meanings as listed by the analyst actually represent different percepts in the communicational system under investigation, or do they represent different ways the investigator or his sources (whether people or reference works) have of translating a foreign range of meaning. In the Pawnee example referred to before, the Pawnee speaker did not have a perceptive difference between the concept of 'paternal aunt' and 'wife." The meaning assigned to the word rests on the fact that English speakers do not equate the two. On the contrary, in fact, in most English-speaking countries marriage to an aunt is regarded as incestuous. The two meanings of *punch,* nevertheless, are real. The structural relationship, technically called *polysemy* ('many meanings') when considered from the cognitive viewpoint, or *homophony* when considered from the manifesting viewpoint, provided the manifestation is phonological, arises from any one of three historical developments:

(1) Loan words similar in form to native words may enter a language.

(2) Originally distinct forms or signals may evolve in converging

fashion until they become identical in their outward manifestation.

(3) A manifesting mark with a protomeaning of some kind may evolve so that new meanings accrue.

The *punch* example represents the first pattern. English, which already had a word *punch* 'blow' or 'stroke,' borrowed another word of like sound from one of the languages of India. This word, derived from Sanskrit, originally meant 'five,' from the number of ingredients in the drink. Now, of course, the beverage may be made from any number.

The words *to* and *two*, although not spelled alike, are phonologically identical. They illustrate the second possibility, convergence, since the first word was *tō* (pronounced like modern English *toe*) in Old English, and the second was *twā*. Despite the current difference in the orthography, which preserves an archaic pattern, eventually they and also the word *too* could come to be spelled alike since they are pronounced alike.

The third possibility, the development of additional and distinct meanings, may be seen in the word *trip* which once meant and still can mean a 'journey' or 'voyage' but has now developed an additional one, referring to 'a state of mind, normally when one is under the influence of narcotic drugs.'

The major problem here is to ascertain whether one is dealing with a true either/or situation or whether the description is a translational convenience but does not reflect perceptive differentiation in the target-system of the analysis. The answer must rest on whether the user of the language—that is, the native speaker—contrasts the different meanings, not whether the analyst does. This information is not difficult to get, but the trained investigator must always keep the important difference firmly in mind if he is to arrive at a true picture of the sociocultural system he is describing.

5.2 Monochronic, Di- or Polysystemic Analysis

How can one compare two or more sociocultural systems in a way that reflects precision of description and actual structuring? The answer, of course, must start with an accurate and precise description of each of the systems under contemplation since one can hardly compare that which has barely been described in its own right. To the extent that an analysis of the perceptual scheme might be carried out independently for two or more communicational systems, one would then have an index of the associated sociocultural systems as seen from the point of view of their own members. A simple juxtaposition and comparison of such percept-inventories would lead to a straightforward index of identities and dissimilarities, one which could even be quantified, since, as pointed out in section 5.1, the degree of integration of percepts into the total system is part of the reflex of that pattern. In comparing two (or more) such systems, one would note the following:

(1) Certain percepts present in System A would be totally lacking in System B.

(2) Certain percepts present in System A would also be present in System B but with the same or a different degree of integration.

If the compared systems should exist at the same time (i.e., be monochronic or synchronic), the comparison index would also be a *compatibility index* and could well serve to predict the interactions of members of the systems. For example, in one American Indian system there is an in-group out-group structuring of some consequence, but within the in-group there is no percept comparable to the Indo-European distinction with reference to possession; there is no 'my' versus 'your' versus 'his' structuring. All members of the in-group have joint ownership. Consequently, one might predict that if an English speaker should somehow be accepted by the in-group and consequently be included in the dinner arrangements, and if he should take off his coat when he sat down to eat, he might —or might not—find it again when he arose. To the extent that such an English speaker would not be bicultural, he would think that someone had stolen his coat. To the Indian who took it, however, the coat was his: that is, a joint possession of all in-group members. He simply put on his own coat; he did not take someone else's, although, of course, the coat continued to belong to the original owner as well as to him. If the same English speaker could comprehend the other system as projected by the percept pattern, he might simply pick up another coat—any coat which struck his fancy, even two if he wished, for the other coats would be his also.

The foregoing example illustrates how the lack of a linguistic reflex of a percept distinction can disclose part of the patterning of the sociocultural system. Conversely, an additional percept, as identified by communicational analysis, would also have its sociocultural reflex, but the exact nature of the correlation would not necessarily be predictable. The fact that the Lardil pattern (discussed in Section 5.1) discriminates generation into 'odds' and 'evens' is patent from even a cursory examination of the language. Yet although one could recognize this perceptual reflex in the family seating arrangements after one had seen them, one would not be able to predict simply by recognizing the percept or even its degree of integration (relatively high) that the percept difference would take (among others) this particular form.

Two or more systems which are not synchronic can be compared in the same way, but one cannot describe such a comparison as a compatibility index other than hypothetically since the members of the different cultures can never be juxtaposed.

5.3 Polychronic, Diasystemic Analysis

The comparison of different periods of the "same" system is a history. Strictly speaking, of course, once any change has taken place, no system is ever quite the same system thereafter, except in a developmental, genetic way. Here too one must start with independent analyses of each of the systems to be compared. Then the subsequent comparison of inventories would reveal those percepts (conceptual distinctions) that had been added and those which had disappeared. In an all-or-nothing dichotomy, the additions reflect the changing sociocultural system more promptly than the losses since these new percepts immediately acquire some manifesting marks at some level in the communicational system, while the sociocultural items which disappear do not necessarily cause the manifestations of the percept to disappear quite as promptly. People still think and speak about the past, and consequently, may retain the manifesting marks with their associated percepts for some time beyond that of the actual existence of the macrosystemic analogues.

Section 2 showed how one could reconstruct a good part of the sociocultural history or any subdivision of it by a sequential dating of the elements being added to the lexicon or those that are obsolescent or obsolete. The goal, of course, is the percept inventory behind the lexicon and not the simple list of vocabulary items. Therefore it should be evident that all manifesting marks are grist for the analytic mill. Most manifesting marks other than those preserved through the writing system normally go unrecorded. Since, however (as also pointed out in Section 2), diachronic reconstruction can proceed through purely synchronic evidence, even gestural or other normally unrecorded manifesting outlets may play a role in historical reconstruction. This possibility will be considered in the next section.

5.4 Diachronic Projection from Synchronic, Polysystemic Analysis

One of the most useful contributions communicational analysis has to offer to historians is the possibility of reconstructing earlier periods even when so-called "direct" documentation is lacking. Yet what may be regarded as direct or indirect is really a matter of interpretation and technique. To the police detective, the fact that no one has directly observed a criminal suspect at the scene of a crime is no obstacle to ultimately proving the culprit's presence at the given place if the latter has left fingerprints. Similarly, the presence synchronically of certain linguistic evidence presupposes certain unalterable historical events which the analyst may rightly take as having been proven just as certainly as if a witness had written down his observations. In fact, this kind of evidence is even sounder as a guide since human observers are notoriously unreliable, even when well trained in observation.

Consider a simple, perhaps self-evident, example. Assuredly one must assume the presence of biological families in the Proto-Indo-European system, with normal genetic relationships such as mothers, fathers, sisters, and brothers. Even if one does not have any direct eyewitness report of this fact, the linguistic "fingerprints" thousands of years old remain as testimony: Latin *fräter*, Old Irish *bráthir*, Gothic *brōþar*, Old Norse *brōþir*, Old High German *bruodar*, Old

English *brōþor* (whence modern English *brother*), Old Church Slavic *bratru*, Sankrit *bhrātar-* (occurring only in combinations), and so on.

Just as one does not need the print of all five fingers to prove the one-time presence of a burglar, since even one clear impression, say of an index finger will do, one does not need the presence of cognate forms in all descendant languages to establish the one-time existence of a word for 'brother' in Proto-Indo-European (from which comes the reasonable inference of the existence of brothers). Even two cognate forms will do, provided they show the appropriate phonological deviations from the assumed, reconstructed prototype, here Indo-European *b^hrāter*. Thus Indo-European b^h remained as such in Indo-Iranian, source of Sanskrit (seen in the *bhrātar-* form), but shifted to *f* in Latin (seen in *frāter*) and to *b* in Germanic (as in Old Norse *brōþir*). Any two such correlations match the regular pattern and, thus presuppose an Indo-European rather than a later origin.

Sometimes, of course, words change their meaning and so the Greek cognate of the foregoing, namely *p^hrāter*, became specialized to signify 'the member of a phratry or brotherhood.' Since the percept itself remained, however, it had to have some manifesting outlet, whence the Greek *adelp^hós* 'brother.' Yet even this word may be traced back to Indo-European, namely to a compound *sm-*, 'single,' plus *g^welb^h-* 'womb,' which is likewise attested in the Sanskrit *sa-garbhya-*. In other words, the replacing form meant 'coming from a single womb.'

The techniques employed in this single illustration allow a total reconstruction of the protosystem, ranging through all of the conceptual areas from kinship terms to agricultural terms, legal terms to religious terms, and so on. The first phase of such an analysis would be the projection of the protolexicon (or other manifesting outlet) with whatever picture it might give of the protosystem. This type of reconstruction—even in a segmental form—can provide a means of cross-checking assertions or assumptions arrived at by other means. For instance, one historian recently asserted that none of the African civilization south of a specific geographical boundary knew the use of the wheel prior to the sixteenth century. A simple check of the words for "wheel" in the various genetically related families (outside of Afro-Asiatic which occurs mainly north of the boundary) reveals no lexical items whose forms permit a reconstruction of the word in the protolinguistic ancestry of these languages. A single pair of cognate forms with the requisite phonological correlations (as in *bhrātar-/frāter*), however, would conclusively disprove the hypothesis.

The second phase of analysis would consider the earlier and later phases of each genetic group, thus leading to a history. As has been suggested, here the central consideration would be change, whether such change involved the addition, the subtraction, or the mutation of percepts. For instance, in the Nilo-Saharan languages one can reconstruct a word for 'lion,' which appears as *muddu* in Saharan (Berti), *amara(k)* in Maban (Maba), *muru* in Fur, and (with the movable *k* prefix that characterizes the group) *kamiru* (Bari) and *kämiru* (Keliko) among other forms in the Chari-Nile branch. Yet the regular and anticipated cognate in Songhai (Djerma dialect) is *mar*, which means 'leopard,' not 'lion.' One may postulate then the following:

(1) The Songhai group migrated westward from the original more easterly homeland.

(2) In the new environment the lion was either unknown or appeared infrequently whereas leopards were found in abundance, hence the shift in meaning from 'lion' to 'leopard.'

The greater importance of the leopard as compared with the lion in this area appears in evidence from another linguistic family, the Afro-Asiatic. On the basis of forms found in most of the major branches of that group, one may postulate a Proto-Afro-Asiatic word for 'lion,' as in the Semitic *'ari* (Hebrew) or *aru:* (Akkadian), the Ancient Egyptian *rw*, the Berber *awar*, or the Cushitic *a:r* (Somali). Yet the meaning of the cognates of the foregoing words in those Chad languages spoken in areas contiguous to that occupied by the Songhai is 'leopard,' as in Zumu *aruwo*, Kumbu *aru*, or Mubi *oruna*. Presumably the Chadic groups likewise migrated to the leopard area after having separated from their Proto-Afro-Asiatic kinsmen who had used the protolexeme to mean 'lion,' not 'leopard.'

The fact that the original meaning was 'lion' rather than 'leopard' is seen from the development of the cognate form in one Chad sublanguage, Gulfei *arfu*, which acquired the meaning 'elephant.'

Having left predominantly lion territory, the entire Chadic group then had had a manifesting unit (the earlier form of the words which originally meant 'lion' and which were to develop to 'leopard' or, aberrantly, to 'elephant') with a meaning no longer central to their needs. Commonly in linguistic systems when manifesting units exist with no function, they eventually either take on a new function (as here), or they disappear. The special though irregular development to the meaning 'elephant,' incidentally, allows an additional obvious inference to be made regarding the territory into which the Gulfei had gone.

The foregoing reconstructions rested on evidence remaining from several different periods, ranging from the Ancient Egyptian of nearly five thousand years ago to the modern languages of Chad, Semitic (Hebrew cited), and so on. Yet all of the forms dated from periods long after the time of the protosystem reconstructed. Furthermore one could adduce the same source form on the basis of only the modern cognates. The requisite phonological correspondence of those words can only reflect common ancestry, pointing to the protoform of so long ago.

Yet if one can trace extant phonological manifesting marks back to a source form no longer extant, there is no reason at all why one can not do the same for other types of manifesting mark. To date no one appears to have even considered this possibility but its feasibility should be self-evident. The study of gestural systems has not yet reached the level of that accorded to phonological or graphological manifesting patterns, but the principles are exactly the same. The main task here will be the assemblage of enough data regarding cognate gestural patterns to permit reconstruction to be attempted. Thus the example given (Sec. 5.1) of the vertical versus the horizontal height-marking signals of Colombian Spanish would be compared with other systems, such as English which lacks the vertical contrast, with a view to discovering whether the differential development was a loss of one signal in the evolution to English or a gain from Proto-Indo-European in some phase of the evolution to Colombian Spanish. This research would require a check in all of the modern descendants of the parent system to see if any other branch has the dichotomy. If so, one would have to assume an earlier existence of the contrastive percepts ('human' versus 'nonhuman').

However, if no branch but Colombian Spanish has it, one would be led to postulate a separate additive development by structural differentiation either in response to a percept-determined need or in response to a contact problem (e.g., interaction with an Amerindian culture such as Chibcha). Although this line of inquiry cannot be pursued here because of lack of the requisite field work, it holds out intriguing possibilities.

6. MONANTHROPICAL RECONSTRUCTION

Sociocultural reconstruction aims, by diverse means, at an analytic statement of the cognitive patterning of the members of a system and, thus, at some insight regarding all or part of the place, time, and circumstances in which the communicators live or once lived. The object of the perception, not the communicator who did the perceiving, constitutes the goal of this type of analysis. Yet any such perception, as encoded into language or other communicational devices, certainly implies a perceiver, and a great amount of information about this perceiver remains fossilized in the message itself. Indeed, under ideal conditions (not always realized in practice), if one had (a) all of the original signals of the message, (b) a complete analytic breakdown of all of the possible manifesting alternatives of that sociocultural system, and (c) a statement of the correlations between the manifesting marks and those segments of society who use them, one would be able to pinpoint unerringly the particular person who had initiated the message. One could specify that person's residence, age, sex, occupation, educational level, ethnic background, and so on in a way that would differentiate him from any other individual who ever lived. One might even be able to make some statement about his personality through an appropriate analysis of the means of signaling, quite apart from the content of the message.

At an intuitive level most people actually do practice some such analysis of those who communicate with them. Thus, for example, if a man were to say, "He don't have no more," some audiences would immediately assess him as ranking relatively low on the scale of formal education. In the word *He,* the presence rather than the absence of the /h/ identifies certain regional varieties of English, and gives a start—even for the nonlinguist—toward the type of geographical triangulation dealt with earlier in this book. How far beyond this point a nonlinguist could take the analysis would depend on his own personal background. The linguist, of course, would simply proceed systematically, noting next the quality of the vowel of *He,* and so forth. It is the intent here, of course, not to perform the analysis *in extenso* but merely to point out the types of information one might look for. Obviously the explicit details applicable to the English of an adult male cab driver in New York City in the current year would hardly apply, say, to the Norman French nobleman of the year 1530. Yet, subject to the problems posed by the loss of some of the information requisite for either analysis, one could place both persons rather accurately in their proper slots in their own systems.

Note that the techniques of monanthropical reconstruction (identification of the individual man) differ fundamentally from those for sociocultural reconstruction. The latter approach takes the cognitive system as the goal of the analysis. With such a frame of reference, it does not matter whether the communicator uses the word *petrol* (British usage) or *gas* (American usage). For the purpose of reconstructing the sociocultural system (rather than the individual in that system), what is central is the fact that the system recognizes as relevant—hence undoubtedly uses—the hydrocarbon fuel, however the concept may be expressed in the manifesting mechanism of the communicational scheme. The reconstruction of the individual communicator's place in his system, on the other hand, depends not on the cognitive scheme (except in the most indirect way) but rather on the differential correlations between the manifesting system and the sociocultural system (e.g., *petrol* correlates with "British" and *gas* correlates with "American"). Such differentiae exist at all linguistic levels, and if there is any sociocultural differentiation at all (e.g., mailman versus physician, mother versus father, club member versus nonmember), the linguistic system will show the marks of the sociocultural distinctions. It is the task of the analyst to assess all relevant communicational features which correlate *differentially* with the sociocultural demarcations.

Actually, the analytic reconstruction of the individual may proceed on more than one level. Every single person, if he is normal, has internalized more than one communicational system. He does not express himself quite the same way under all circumstances. He uses one pattern in formal situations, a different one in informal situations; one pattern when addressing a social superior, another when addressing an equal, and a third when addressing a social inferior; and so on. It must be realized that each of these differentiae is an independent, crosscutting variable which is itself a subpart of a larger pattern. Thus the manifesting-mark evidence—to the extent that it is available—divides into two hierarchal levels: (*a*) the intersystemic and (*b*) the intrasystemic.

The first, the intersystemic, reflects the fact that every individual is definable analytically as the sum total of all of the parameters which differentiate human beings from each other (i.e., his age, sex, occupation, etc.). He must differ from absolutely every other human being by at least one parameter and normally by more than one. That is, individual *A* is older than individual *B;* individual *A* is a physician, and individual *B* is a plumber; and so forth. Every dfferentiating—and defining—sociocultural feature of this kind has some communicational analogue. For example, to take a lexical difference which reflects the occupational background, where the plumber would say "calf muscle," the physician would be more precise, specifying "gastrocnemius" or "soleus." Where the plumber would say "knee," the physician might say "patella." Indeed, to some extent, it is likely that the plumber would not even understand much of the technical jargon employed by the physician, e.g., "The pterygoideus internus arises from the medial surface of the lateral pterygoid plate, the pyramidal process of the palatine bone, and the tuberosity of the maxilla." Likewise, of course, the reverse might hold true, that is, the plumber's special jargon would not be used by or even be intelligible to the physician. However if the latter had had some plumbing experience, this background itself would be part of the bundle of relevant sociocultural features defining this particular individual, and his use of language would reflect that fact in some appropriate way.

To repeat then, the intersystemic features are those which differentiate individuals from one another. These features are actually part of the entire macrosociocultural matrix and are not linguistic or communicative as such, but, as indicated, they have their reflections in the manifesting part of the communicative scheme and, thus, may serve as diagnostic cues. Every single sociocultural feature of this matrix which defines the individual then leaves its trace in the communicative scheme, and therefore, if the analyst identifies each of the communicative (manifesting-mark) clues pointing to the sociocultural parameters, he is actually building a composite sketch of the person to be identified much as the police artist may put together information about each of the features of a suspect until he has a close approximation of the actual image.

The intrasystemic parameters are those which define the different states or contexts of the same individual (who has already been defined as against other individuals by the intersystemic parameters). Thus, as suggested above, anger versus calmness, formality versus informality, superiority versus inferiority with respect to a particular audience, and many more features (*a*) define the state of the individual at a given time and in a given context and (*b*) dictate the choice of communicational signals from the entire range available to that particular individual. One should note that each particular individual has available to him and to him alone a specific set of possible patterns. Although there necessarily is some overlap, the total set of patterns differs from individual to individual: *the intrasystemically-defined set associated with any given intersystemic bundle differs from that associated with another intersystemic bundle.* For example, the speech pattern of a college teacher of English differs from that of a truck driver (all other relevant parameters being equal). Each has an intrasystemic pattern utilized under conditions of stress or anger, yet the means each employs to signal the anger would normally differ. The truck driver would, among other devices, employ certain lexical items often euphemistically called "four-letter-words." The English teacher would express the same anger not by obscenities but by a markedly different pattern of stress and intonation and by employing forms generally associated with extreme formality (e.g., "*Mr.* Smith" instead of "Bob").

In effect then, every total bundle of sociocultural parameters defining a particular person in a specific relevant context correlates with a unique set of communicative devices. To the extent that the communicative pattern (or partial pattern) has been correctly correlated with a given set of sociocultural parameters (inter- and intrasystemic), one can reconstruct (*a*) the place of the particular individual in his own setting and (*b*) something, at least, of what he regarded as critical in the particular context in which he delivered his message. There are two major obstacles to this procedure:

(1) Sometimes the sample of raw data is too short to include the differential information required.

(2) Not all sociocultural parameters have been either identified or correlated with their associated communicative reflexes.

The first obstacle is merely one of the degree or extent to which the analytic breakdown is possible. Even the shortest message conceivable contains at least some differential information, either negative or positive. Thus a single "Yes" would contrast, say, with "Yeah" or "Yup" or various other possibilities on both the inter- and intrasystemic scales. If actually pronounced rather than written, the "Yes" would further differentiate still other correlations by means of a variety of articulations, from the more common /jɛs/ to /jɪs/, /jɛɪs/, or even /jɛjas/, the last-mentioned form restricted to specific areas of the southern United States. Every additional message element would provide further corroborative or else cross-cutting segmentations until, under ideal circumstances, every demarcative parameter had been identified with the subsequent identification of the specific communicator himself, together with his circumstances when framing this particular message. Obviously the single-word affirmation can provide only the barest start toward the triangulation process, but, as suggested, it does provide some differential information.

Typical intersystemic parameters in English and many genetically related sociocultural patterns are the following:

(1) Geography
(2) Age of the individual
(3) Age of the language at the period used
(4) Sex
(5) Occupation
(6) Ethnic background
(7) Level of education

The extent to which these and other differentiae are embedded in the communication matrix varies from system to system and from period to period. Among the Ainu, for example, at each of a number of relevant ages, the communicator switches patterns and uses a lexicon which is different from that which he used at an earlier phase of his life. It marks him as having come to the age in question.

English has communicational features which differentiate the sexes: particular lexical items which are normal for women but would mark a male as effeminate if he were to employ them, as well as the reverse; intonational patterns that differ in certain respects (quite apart from the natural pitch-range distinctions based on the size of the vocal folds); and even specific syntactic differences, only now beginning to be mapped by some investigators. Yet these differences are trivial as compared to those of some systems in which the men and women speak virtually different languages. This greater communicational differentiation mirrors the greater role differentiation of the macrosocioculture itself. The sensitivity of the communicational pattern to the sociocultural matrix appears evident from recent developments of English-speaking peoples where the role-differentiation of males and females has been markedly reduced. Thus, coextensive with the increased occupational mobility and aspirations of women, which now parallel those of men in more ways than formerly, is the quite open employment by women of linguistic practices once forbidden them—among others, for example, the use of obscene language. Just a generation ago a woman would have been regarded as unsexed and a subject of horror had she dared to use the language many women regularly employ today.

Intrasystemic parameters, that is, those features marking the different relevant context-determined patterns of the communicator, include the following:

(1) Relative position in the social scale with respect to any particular audience

(2) Degree of formality

(3) Psychological state (i.e., anger-versus-nonanger scale, enthusiasm-versus-apathy scale, etc.)

Some systems, particularly many of those found in Asia, have complicated deference/honorific mechanisms reflecting a greater sociocultural stratification, one in which every person stands at a certain level in the total evaluative scale with respect to every other person. Thus one would signify one's own inferiority, equality, or superiority with respect to the audience by appropriate modes of address, the use of specific, contrastive verbal forms, and so on. As will be discussed (with a different point in view) in a later section of this book, English once signified similar inferiority-superiority relationships by the use of particular pronominal choices (i.e., *thou* versus *ye*) until the sociocultural restructuring itself (to be analyzed) caused the elimination of its linguistic reflex. Yet even some varieties of Modern English still retain mechanisms that permit the contrasts to be made, as in the peremptory command "Open the window!" uttered to a social inferior versus "Would you kindly open the window?" uttered to a superior. Distinctive intonational patterns not indicated in the writing system convey additional nuances. Since these and other communicational choices reflect noncommunicational situations, they may be utilized as clues, enabling the analyst to backtrack from the communicational evidence to the reconstruction of the relevant features of the situation in which the communication took place.

NOTES

The first general analysis of the entire range of inter- and intrasystemic patterns will appear in L. G. Heller and James Macris, *Usage and Style*, soon to be published by Holt, Rinehart and Winston. Thus far, for most languages differential analysis of the type suggested has focused predominantly on geographically determined features, although sporadic studies clearly demonstrate the feasibility of distinguishing other sociocultural elements. The literature on geolinguistics, however, is quite extensive for all of the major languages of the world. No attempt will be made here to give a complete bibliography, which, because of the number of languages concerned, would require many volumes. The following list of works on English alone represents just a small, though selective, sampling designed to suggest the scope of the field.

Allen, Harold B. "Minor Dialect Areas of the Upper Midwest," *Publication of the American Dialect Society*, No. 30 (Nov., 1958), pp. 3-16.
———. "Canadian-American Speech Differences Along the Middle Border," *Journal of the Canadian Linguistic Association*, V, i (Spring, 1959), 17-24.
Atwood, E. B. "A Preliminary Report on Texas Word Geography," *Orbis*, II (Jan., 1953), 61-66.

————. *A Survey of Verb Forms in the Eastern United States.* Ann Arbor: University of Michigan Press, 1953.

————. *The Regional Vocabulary of Texas.* Austin: University of Texas Press, 1962.

————. "The Methods of American Dialectology," *Zeitschrift fur Mundart-forschung,* XXX (Oct., 1963), 1-30.

Avis, Walter S. "The Mid-Back Vowels in the English of the Eastern United States: A Detailed Investigation of Regional and Social Differences in Phonic Characteristics and Phonemic Organization." Doctoral Dissertation, University of Michigan, 1956; microfilm.

————. "Speech Differences Above the Ontario-United States Border," *Journal of the Canadian Linguistic Association,* I, i (Oct., 1954), 13-17; I, i (Regular Series, March, 1956), 14-19; II, ii (Oct., 1956), 41-59.

Babington, Mima, and E. B. Atwood. "Lexical Usage in Southern Louisiana," *Publication of the American Dialect Society,* No. 36 (Nov., 1961), pp. 1-24.

Barrows, S. T. "Watch, Water, Water, Wash," *American Speech,* IV (April, 1929), 301-302.

Baugh, Albert C. *A History of the English Language.* New York: Appleton-Century-Crofts, 1957. Note especially pp. 228-231 for the Middle English dialects and pp. 436-446 for the Modern American English dialects.

Berger, Marshall D. "Accent, Pattern, and Dialect in North American English," *Word* 24 (1968), 55-61.

Brengelman, F. H. "The Native American English Spoken in the Puget Sound Area," Doctoral dissertation, University of Washington, 1957.

Clough, W. O. "Some Wyoming Speech Patterns," *American Speech,* XXIX (Feb., 1954), 28-35.

Davis, A. L. "A Word Atlas of the Great Lakes Region." Doctoral dissertation, University of Michigan, 1948.

DeCamp, David. "The Pronunciation of English in San Francisco," *Orbis,* VII (June, 1958), 372-391; VIII (Jan., 1959), 54-77.

Duckert, Audrey R. "The Linguistic Atlas of New England Revisited," *Publication of the American Dialect Society,* No. 39 (April, 1963), pp. 8-15.

Dunbar, Gary S. "A Southern Geographical Word List," *American Speech,* XXXVI (Dec., 1961), 293-296.

Francis, W. Nelson. "Regional Variety in English," *The English Language: An Introduction.* New York: W. W. Norton & Company, Inc., 1965.

Hankey, Clyde T. "A Colorado Word Geography," *Publication of the American Dialect Society,* No. 34 (Nov., 1960).

Hubbell, Allan F. *The Pronunciation of English in New York City.* New York: Kings Crown Press, 1950.

Kimmerle, M. M., R. I. McDavid, Jr., and V. G. McDavid. "Problems of Linguistic Geography in the Rocky Mountain Area," *Western Humanities Review,* V (Summer, 1951), 249-264.

Kurath, Hans. *Handbook of the Linguistic Geography of New England.* Providence: Brown University Press, 1939.

———. *A Word Geography of the Eastern United States.* Ann Arbor: University of Michigan Press, 1949.

———, and R. I. McDavid, Jr. *The Pronunciation of English in the Atlantic States.* Ann Arbor: University of Michigan Press, 1961.

McDavid, R. I., Jr. "Linguistic Geography in Canada: An Introduction," *Journal of the Canadian Linguistic Association,* I, i (Oct., 1954), 3-8.

———, and V. G. McDavid, "Grammatical Differences in the North Central States," *American Speech,* XXXV (Feb., 1960), 5-19.

———. "Regional Linguistic Atlases in the United States," *Orbis,* V (June, 1956), 349-386.

McDavid, V. G. "Verb Forms in the North-Central States and the Upper Midwest." Doctoral dissertation, University of Minnesota, 1956; microfilm.

Marcwardt, A. H. "Middle English *o* in American English of the Great Lakes Area." *Papers of the Michigan Academy of Science,* XXVI (1941), 561-571.

———. "Middle English *wa* in the speech of the Great Lakes Region," *American Speech,* XVII (Dec., 1942), 226-234.

———. "Principal and Subsidiary Dialect Areas in the North-Central States," *Publication of the American Dialect Society,* No. 27 (April, 1957), pp. 3-15.

———. *American English.* New York: Oxford University Press, Inc., 1958.

Mills, R. V. "Oregon Speechways," *American Speech,* XXV (May 1950), 81-90.

O'Hare, Thomas J. "The Linguistic Geography of Eastern Montana," Doctoral dissertation, University of Texas, 1964; microfilm.

Orton, Harold, and Eugen Dieth. *Survey of English Dialects.* Leeds: E. J. Arnold and Son, Ltd., 1962-.

Pearce, T. M. "Three Rocky Mountain Terms: park, sugar plaza," *American Speech,* XXXIII (May, 1958), 99-107.

Pyles, Thomas. *Words and Ways of American English.* New York: Random House, Inc., 1952.

———. "The Pronunciation of English in the State of Washington," *American Speech,* XXVII (Oct., 1952), 186-189.

———. "Washington Words," *Publication of the American Dialect Society,* No. 25 (April, 1956), pp. 3-11.

———. "Word Geography of the Pacific Northwest," *Orbis* VI (Jan.-June, 1957), 82-89.

———. "The Pronunciation of English in the Pacific Northwest," *Language,* XXVII (Oct.-Dec., 1961), 559-564.

Reed, Carroll E. *Dialects of American English.* Cleveland and New York: The World Publishing Company, 1967.

Reed, D. W. "Eastern Dialect Words in California," *Publication of the American Dialect Society.* No. 21 (April, 1954), pp. 3-15.

Shuy, Roger W. *Discovering American Dialects.* Champaign, Illinois: *National Council of Teachers of English,* 1967.

Thomas, C. K. "The Dialectal Significance of the Non-Phonemic Low-Back Vowel Variants Before *R*," in *Studies in Speech and Drama in Honor of Alexander M. Drummond.* Ithaca, New York, 1944.

———. "Notes on the Pronunciation of 'Hurry,'" *American Speech,* XXI (April, 1946), 114.

———. *An Introduction to the Phonetics of American English,* 2nd ed. New York: The Ronald Press Company, 1958.

Turner, L. D. "Notes on the Sounds and Vocabulary of Gullah," *Publication of the American Dialect Society,* No. 3 (May, 1945) pp. 13-28.

———. "Problems Confronting the Investigator of Gullah,'" *Publication of the American Dialect Society,* No. 9 (April, 1948), pp. 74-84.

Wetmore, Thomas H. "The Low-Central and Low-Back Vowels in the English of the Eastern United States," *Publication of the American Dialect Society,* No. 32 (Nov., 1959).

Wood, Gordon R. "An Atlas Survey of the Interior South (U.S.A.)," *Orbis,* IX (Jan., 1960), 7-12.

———. "Word Distribution in the Interior South," *Publication of the American Dialect Society,* No. 35 (April, 1961), 1-16.

Wyld, Henry C. *A Short History of English,* 2nd ed. London: John Murray, 1921.

Considerations of time and space prohibit an attempt at a bibliography for all languages, either for purely geolinguistic listings or for listings of studies of any of the other linguistic correlates of the remaining sociocultural determinants. The Annual Bibliography of the Modern Language Association is a useful reference source for tracking down work done in any of the areas. Studies of the particular languages normally appear in the initial (linguistic) section under the headings of the languages. This *M.L.A. Bibliography* appeared as a single issue once each year through 1969. From 1970 on, the section *General Linguistics* has appeared as a volume by itself, separate from other bibliographical listings.

7. GRAPHOLOGICAL RECONSTRUCTION

Hindsight, it has been said, is usually better than foresight. This maxim holds strikingly true in many fields: today's dullest beginning student often knows far more and is capable of solving infinitely more problems than even the greatest of the pioneers in many areas. The early scholars had to find their own way, step by step, often with missteps or digressions into blind alleys, groping to discover answers, which, in retrospect, appear self-evident. Frequently the explorer in terra incognita does not even know what it is that he has discovered. He himself may not be in a position to assess his own work or make the generalized observations which will eventually light the way for those who follow.

The tales of the great decipherments read like strange combinations of fairy tales and detective stories, intertwined with romance and adventure—Henry Rawlinson dangling over a 2,000 foot cliff at Behustan in order to copy the Old Persian cuneiform inscriptions; Alice Kober in her vain race to solve the mystery of the linear inscriptions of ancient Greece before death would claim her, but, nevertheless, setting the stage for her successor, Michael Ventris, to take the last step a scant two years later; young Champollion frantic at the thought that someone other than he might have solved the secrets of the Rosetta Stone, with its tantalizing hieroglyphic writing. Each of these tales deserves a book, and, indeed, such books have been and still are being written, usually for their high excitement and wonder in the quest for the unknown. Nonetheless, this book aims at disclosing the methodology employed and so must eschew part of the human drama in order to focus on the lessons that may be gathered from the often intuitive, hit-or-miss efforts of the great decipherers.

7.1 A Glossographic Typology

The actual history of the decipherments of writing systems, quite apart from the human values just alluded to, presents a picture of false starts, misguided activities, occasional insights, and, in general, endless miscellaneous details of all sorts, with little order or direction. A series of relevant questions, however, aimed at setting up a general typology of all possible problems related to decipherments may perhaps reduce the chaotic array to an orderly, comprehensive pattern. At the most fundamental level, two questions would appear to be primary:

(1) What is known about the language represented by the script?

(2) What is known about the writing system itself?

These are independent questions, since one may have information about either without reference to the other. Accordingly, Section 7.11 will deal with the former question; and 7.12, with the latter.

7.11 The Language

Regardless of the script and even regardless of the internal structure of the language represented, one may have two general kinds of information about the language, reflected in the following questions:

(1) Can the language of the script be identified? That is, does one know what particular language is represented by the writing?

(2) Is the language of the script—whether identified or not—one that is known, in the sense of understanding, not classification? That is, has the language been described? If so, to what extent and how accurately? Can anyone speak it or interpret it?

The scholars who first attempted to decipher the hieroglyphic writings of ancient Egypt were capable of identifying the language with which they were trying to deal. In fact, they even knew—here in the sense of being able to translate—Coptic, a later version of the same language, but one thousands of years removed. Although an important phase of the decipherment necessarily centered on the values of the written symbols, this phase by itself was not enough. Even if the ancient Egyptian language had been transcribed into a modern notational system known to everyone, it still would have been relatively incomprehensible. The grammar and the lexicon were unknown when the first investigators took up the problem.

On the other hand, the ancient Greek language was well known to scholars in the year 1952. Yet up to that time only a couple of investigators—not including Michael Ventris, the one who ultimately solved the riddle of the writing system itself—even suspected that the Linear B writing found on the clay tablets of Crete, Pylos, and Mycenae was used to transcribe Greek. In fact, Sir Arthur Evans, the discoverer of the tablets first encountered in 1900 at Knossos (Crete), was so convinced that the language was not Greek that he actually exerted his influence to bar from excavations in the field those scholars who disagreed. Ventris, who had originally heard of the tablets from Evans, never even imagined the real truth until he himself finally hit upon the phonological values of symbols and substituted them in the inscriptions, with the results that are now history. Once the phonological values were known, there were thousands of classicists all over the world who were quite capable of reading the tablets. Yet the starting points for the hieroglyphic and the Linear-B decipherments were vastly different. In the former, scholars knew what language was involved, but they did not know the language itself. In the latter, they knew the language but did not associate the tablets with that language.

In actual fact, the two language questions—that of simple identification and that of deeper understanding—really pose a fourfold typological scheme:

(1) Languages identified and known

(2) Languages identified but not known (e.g., ancient Egyptian)

(3) Languages not identified but known (e.g., the Greek of the Linear B tablets)

(4) Languages not identified and not known

Where the language is both identified and known, the problem of decipherment is so simple that it hardly rises beyond the level of a parlor game. Indeed thousands of people while away the hours with activities of precisely this sort provided by magazines devoted to acrostics and other word-play puzzles. If one has enough textual material, the distribution of symbols should follow that usually found for the language as a whole. Hence straight frequency counts of recurrent features suffice for the decoding. For example, the words *and* and *the* are the two most frequent lexical items in most consecutive texts of English. If English were written with some other system, say the hieroglyphic, a count of characters would turn up the fact that two sequences of three different characters appeared with very great frequency. Since the *a* and *e* symbols are among the most frequent single characters in English, their hieroglyphic equivalents would likewise turn up among the highest in frequency distribution. Since, furthermore, *a* has a higher word-initial distribution and *e* a higher word-final distribution, one would be able to ascertain which set of three characters represented *and* and which the word *the*. Given this word identification, one would be led to assign values to the symbols for *n, d, t* and *h*. These values then would be projected for other words (e.g., for *had, tan, at*). This particular problem, although very much oversimplified here (the language might, for example, be written in a nonalphabetic system), poses no real difficulties once the type of writing system has been determined. The problems of the writing systems themselves, however, will be handled in the next section (7.12).

When the language of the unknown writing system is identified but not known, there are varying degrees of difficulty, once the problem of the writing system itself has been solved. If—as for ancient Egyptian—the language belongs to a family of genetically related languages, information about possible cognate equations can be brought to bear on the interpretation. If—again as for the Egyptian—a later version of the language is known, the information about the descendant often provides insight, although it must be used with care. Sometimes the nature of the writing system itself provides helpful clues. These too will be handled under the section on writing systems.

Where the language is a known one but has not been identified as that known language, the investigator must of course center his efforts on the analysis of the writing system. He cannot, prior to the correct assignment of values to the symbols, know whether the problem belongs to class 3 or class 4. He must handle both varieties alike until he has some clue that may identify the language.

When the language is both unknown and unidentified, the order of difficulty of decipherment is highest, but the problem is not insoluble.

7.12 The Writing System

All writing systems may be classified into a general typology according to the kinds of symbols they employ, regardless of the actual shapes of the symbols or of the materials on which or by means of which the symbols are written. Sometimes the materials employed for writing play a role in determining the appearance of the symbols, as will be discussed later, but of far greater consequence is the communicative strategy behind the use of the symbols. The following outline will serve as a guide to the discussion which follows:

I. Primary Symbols
    A. Ideotypic
        1. Pictographic
        2. Nonpictographic
    B. Phonotypic
        1. Syllabic
        2. Alphabetic
        3. Other

II. Secondary Symbols
    A. Ideotypic Disambiguative
        1. Pictographic
        2. Nonpictographic
    B. Phonotypic Disambiguative
        1. Syllabic
        2. Alphabetic
        3. Other

The major dichotomy in the schematization is that between primary and secondary systems. The latter are employed mainly to reinforce the former or to clarify points at which the primary systems fail. The discussion, therefore, will focus first on primary types of symbols.

All written symbols are either ideotypic or phonotoypic, or both. Ideotypic symbols represent ideas directly. Phonotypic symbols stand for units of sound. The ideotypic symbols can be translated into the sounds associated with the ideas represented, but they need not be. Furthermore one can grasp the idea behind the symbol even without knowing the language involved (that is, without either identifying the language or being able to translate it). A picture of a horse or a man, if identifiable as such, can be read directly. The phonic form into which the reader would put the concept necessarily would vary according to his own background. A Greek of the fifth century B.C. might say *hippos* and *ánthropos* while an American of the twentieth century A.D. would say *horse* and *man* (i.e., /hors/ and /mæn/). Most writing systems contain at least some ideotypic symbols. Modern English, for instance, has the numerals 1, 2, 3, 4, and so on. A Spaniard could read these symbols *uno, dos, tres, cuatro,* while a Frenchman might read them *un, deux, trois, quatre,* and the speaker of some other language could read them in still another way. Some writing systems, such as the Chinese, are predominantly ideotypic. This means that the speakers of different Chinese languages—communicative systems which are no longer mutually intelligible to the speakers of genetically but distantly related branches—can read the writing of any other user of this script. The speaker of Cantonese can read and understand the writings of a speaker of Mandarin despite the fact that he cannot converse with the same speaker. This direct tie between the symbol and the concept has played an important role in the reading and deciphering of many systems.

Ideotypic symbols may be either pictographic or nonpictographic. Probably all or most start out as pictures of the object or idea represented, but this picture becomes altered in the course of ages either by virtue of the desire to save time in writing or because of some restriction or difficulty related to the type of materials used in the writing. The early Germanic tribes picked up their knowledge of writing from other peoples but they lacked a ready source of papyrus or of finished parchment on which to write. Consequently they utilized wood or stone, and really carved their symbols. The grain of the wood necessarily meant that chance horizontal lines would appear on any message; therefore horizontal strokes of the earlier symbols were shifted to diagonal strokes, to preclude ambiguity. Likewise the hardness of the surface made curved lines too difficult to handle; hence a shift to only straight lines for the early Germanic runic writing. The system directly handed down to the later speakers of Germanic languages, however, was a late version of the Roman alphabet, borrowed in preference to the runic writing, but only after different materials had become available.

Most of the cuneiform writing systems of the Near East (wedge-shaped characters incised on clay) contain ideotypic symbols, a fact which made all of the languages so written at least partly accessible to anyone who could read the cuneiform of any other of the many types in use. The word for 'god,' for instance, was /ilu/ in Akkadian (a Northeast Semitic language), /siuni/ in Hittite (an Indo-European language), and /dingir/ in Sumerian (a language of no known genetic affinities but attested in writing earlier than any other language unless some recent discoveries in Romania antedate the Sumerian tablets). Each of the languages employed the same sign, however it may have been read. The early version of Sumerian cuneiform shows that the original source of the symbol was a picture of a star. The evolution down to later Sumerian writing so changed this picture, however, that only the professional historian of writing can be aware of the development from a simple pictographic ideotype to the later nonpictographic version employed to represent the idea of 'deity' or 'god' in various languages.

Phonotypic symbols represent sounds or groups of sounds. These sounds, of course, can be—and normally are—associated with ideas, but the phonotypes, *as phonotypes,* do not represent the ideas directly. This type of correlation means that the symbols used to represent the sounds of one language can be borrowed to represent the sounds of another language. The Etruscans, who lived on the Italian Peninsula, used a script quite similar to that of the Romans, who, indeed, may have borrowed the system from the former group, their immediate geographical neighbors. Thus, since modern scholars know the Roman alphabet and since, by means of Latin renderings of Etruscan words and vice versa, they know all of the phonological values of the Etruscan symbols, they can read the script with ease—the word *read* here being used in the sense of 'articulate aloud,' not of 'comprehend.' The situation is analogous to that of an English-speaking student of Hebrew—a well-known language—learning the script but ceasing to take lessons at that point: he then would be able to pronounce the Hebrew text at sight but still would not know the meanings of the words. The analogy goes no further, however, since the student of Hebrew could pick up a grammar and a dictionary of that language to supplement his lack of information. There are no comparable dictionaries or grammars of Etruscan, although in the last few years some progress has been made toward comprehending its structure and affinities. In a similar fashion, scholars know the phonological values of the Meroitic language of Africa and, therefore, can pronounce the texts aloud, but they do not know the meaning of the material.

Phonotypic symbols may represent either individual phonemes or combinations of phonemes. In theory at least, they can even represent distinctive features, elements below the phonemic level, but in practice this possibility can generally be ruled out for ancient writing systems. The Linear B script of Crete was a syllabic type; that is, each symbol stood for an entire syllable. Thus the Greek word for 'tripod' had to be written ∧ ⅄ ⅂ ※ with the first symbol ∧ standing for *ti;* the second, ⅄, for *-ri-;* the third, ⅂ , for *-po/;* and the last, ※ , for *-de.* In such a syllabic system *tri-* could not have been written with a simple *t* before the *r* since there were no purely consonantal signs in the syllabary: every symbol stood either for a vowel or for a consonant plus a vowel. More complex syllable structures do exist, but were not present in the Linear B pattern. Consonant clusters of the *tr-* type were handled by the convention of choosing the syllabic symbol of the first element so that the vowel not to be pronounced was the same as that in the following syllable. Here, then, the first *i* (incorporated in the ∧ *ti-* symbol) was the same as the *i* of the next syllable (incorporated in the ⅄ *-ri* symbol) and, by convention, was understood to be nonfunctional. Should an actual phonological *tiri-* sequence have occurred, the insertion of an extra vocalic symbol after the *ti-* would have cleared up the ambiguity (i.e., *ti-i-ri-*).

The ideal nonsyllabic phonotypic writing system has a one-symbol-to-one-phoneme correlation, but some such phonotypic systems do not indicate all phonemes. By and large, early versions of most of the Semitic writing systems indicated only consonants but not vowels. Since the choice of vowels or even the absence of any vowel at all sometimes signaled important grammatical or other information, this type of writing system occasionally offers alternative possible interpretations of the same text.

Many writing systems of antiquity developed slowly and laboriously; hence several types coexisted side by side in the practice of the same group of scribes. Also certain backup systems were superadded in the efforts to clarify the meaning of the often ambiguous primary systems. For example, the symbol for 'sun,' perhaps originally a simple circle in the ideotypic pictographic phase, could be read directly as the indigenous word for 'sun,' say *Rā* in Ancient Egyptian, but occasionally the same symbol might be employed to mean 'day' or 'shine' or 'bright,' whence arose some likelihood of misreading. To preclude such a possibility one could add either another ideotypic symbol—perhaps here one denoting 'time'—or a phonotypic symbol to give some clue to which of the words was intended. Occasionally, as actually happened in the Ancient Egyptian system, both backup (or disambiguative) systems were employed. Obviously, secondary systems of this kind can display the full range of possibilities of the primary systems: pictographic or nonpictographic ideotypic, or syllabic or alphabetical phonotypic, and so on.

One of the problems, which may seem almost trivial in retrospect but which seriously impeded the initial stages of decipherment of a number of scripts, is that of the direction of the writing. Clearly, no decipherment can take place with any degree of accuracy until this direction is ascertained. If English, for instance, were written ideotypically, the sentence *John hit Paul* might be read *Paul hit John* if the wrong sequence were assumed. If the script in question were written by any of the phonotypic possibilities, the wrong choice of sequence normally would result in phonological combinations that would make no sense at all. Such a mistake was made in the first attempts to decipher the Egyptian hieroglyphics. In general, as regards the direction of writing systems, the dictum "Whatever can happen, does happen" holds true. The following outline indicates some of the major possibilities actually attested:

    I.   Horizontal
        A. Left to right
        B. Right to left
        C. Boustrophedon

    II. Vertical
         A. Top to bottom
         B. Bottom to top
    III. Circular (or Spiral)

The left-to-right system is that seen in English, Latin, or Classical Greek. The Semitic languages such as Hebrew and Arabic follow the right-to-left pattern. Very early Greek and very early stages
of Ancient Egyptian are of the boustrophedon type, namely starting
either at the right or the left, proceeding to the other side, returning
again, and so on—literally 'ox-turning,' the pattern seen in plowing,
where the furrow is made from one side to the other side and then
back. Chinese exemplifies the top-to-bottom pattern; and Nubian,
the bottom-to-top. The Phaistos disk of Ancient Crete (generally
dated as around 1600-1700 B.C.) illustrates a spiral pattern. Whether
the spiral starts at the center and moves outward or on the outside
and moves inward remains uncertain since this clay disk, which, incidentally, is probably the first example of printing from movable
type, is still undeciphered. I. J. Gelb of the University of Chicago
assumes an outside-to-inside arrangement, since many pictographic
writing systems have the pictures facing the beginning of the line.
One might reasonably dispute this assumption on two grounds: (*a*)
some writing systems show the pictures facing the direction of writing, and (*b*), of greater consequence, human planning is imperfect.
If the scribe had started on the outside, it is highly unlikely that he
would have ended precisely at the center. He would either have
finished his message too soon, leaving a blank space before the center,
or he would have been forced to continue the message on the back
or on another disk. If he had started in the center, he could have
added as much extra clay to the outside as needed to complete the
message. Neither side of the single disk containing this ancient printing shows any space at all around the center. Both sides, however, do
show a brief space at the end of the outside sequence of figures.

Returning to the problem of the full range of directional possibilities, one could hypothesize additional schemes since the reading
of horizontal lines of any of the three types could itself proceed
from top to bottom or bottom to top. Likewise, the reading of
vertical columns could as well proceed from left to right as from

right to left. Also the vertical arrangement could be written in boustrophedon fashion; or, within a line, some symbols could be arranged vertically with respect to each other although the predominant direction were horizontal. These and other possibilities are self-evident once one is aware of the importance of recognizing the problem.

As suggested by the comments on the Phaistos-disk puzzle, one way of ascertaining the direction would be the location of blank spaces at the end of a line. In English, of course, indentation signals paragraphing, but initial indentations of this kind are of uniform length, whereas, because of the variability of message lengths, the size of the spaces at the end of such paragraphs is not uniform, whence one would be led to assume that the irregularly spaced blanks represent terminal points of segments of a message. Given the terminus, one can then ascertain the normal direction of symbols, from which can be recognized a horizontal sequence from the left or the right, a vertical sequence from top or bottom, or a boustrophedon progression.

An additional problem is that of the segmentation of meaningful sequences of symbols. English does this by means of spacing between words, as did many ancient systems. Others separated segments by means of strokes or, as in the Phaistos disk, by outlining. Occasionally, however, all symbols are simply run together with no separation at all.

7.2 General Observations Regarding Decipherment

Even if the language of the script to be translated is both unidentified and unknown, the actual interpretation can nevertheless proceed provided the writing system is either partially or totally of the pictographic ideotypic variety and at least some of the symbols correlate with meanings in the would-be translator's conceptual system. Of course, one must constantly keep in mind the fact that some percepts of the target system would necessarily be missed, misinterpreted, or distorted because of differences between that target system and the one of the translator. As will be recalled from the earlier discussion, the concept of 'father,' for instance, is not the same for a Pawnee speaker as for an English speaker since their sociocultural systems are markedly different. Nevertheless the picture of a horse or of a man, if recognizable as such, does convey some conceptualization. Pictures of concrete objects, as may be expected, are more readily identifiable than abstract ideas.

The translation can also proceed if the writing system contains nonpictographic ideotypic symbols, provided this particular variety of symbols is already known from some other language for which they were once employed. The cuneiform systems of a number of Near Eastern languages employed identical or similar ideotypic symbols which could be read translinguistically, thus facilitating some of the decipherments.

If the writing system is not of the ideotypic variety, however, one must have at least some means of assigning meanings to the symbols or groups of symbols. With the Ancient Egyptian hieroglyphics this problem was solved partly by comparing the earlier version of the language used in the unknown writing system with later known versions of the same language, as well as with cognate languages of the same genetic family. Furthermore, initially, a trilingual key had been provided in the form of the Rosetta Stone containing inscriptions in two versions of Egyptian, both unknown, and in Classical Greek, which was readily understandable to thousands of classicists. Hence one had a direct, but not word-for-word, translation.

The simple provision of a textual translation is an important aid, but it does not in itself constitute a decipherment since it leaves many problems unsolved. More will be said about this situation later. In a number of decipherments, short inscriptions on tools such as axes and knives were presumed to contain the words for such implements inasmuch as the same sets of symbols appeared repeatedly on different axes and knives. Thus, for instance, Hans Bauer, the Semiticist who deciphered the Ugaritic cuneiform writing system discovered in 1929 at Ras Shamrah, Syria, made a shrewd guess that the four recurring symbols which appeared on a number of bronze axes must be the word for 'axe.'

Such guesses, although fortunate and useful for the assignment of possible phonological values to phonotypic symbols, hardly constitute a lexicon or grammar. Scholars have been more fortunate in other instances such as the discovery of actual dictionaries compiled in antiquity. The ancient Babylonians, who wrote and spoke an East Semitic language, had retained the archaic Sumerian language for religious purposes, much as Latin has been preserved in Roman Catholic rituals or Hebrew in Jewish synagogues, whatever country the Jews or Catholics may have lived or settled in and whatever other languages they may use in everyday life. Since the Babylonian scribes did not know Sumerian as a native language, they had to learn it as a foreign one, whence stemmed the compilation of glossaries and dictionaries of cuneiform, as used in each language. This kind of fortunate discovery is extremely rare.

When the writing system is neither a pictographic ideotypic one nor a known nonpictographic ideotypic variety, and one has no immediate extensive translation key, either in the form of a dictionary, as for Sumerian, or of a dual or multiple inscriptional type, the attack on the problem must focus on the writing system itself. Here a simple count of the number of symbols immediately sorts the range of possibilities into three distinct classes:

(1) If there are fewer than forty symbols, the script is almost certain to be an alphabetic, phonotypic system. English, for instance uses twenty-six characters; Hebrew, twenty-two; Ugaritic, thirty.

(2) If the number of characters should range from eighty to one hundred, the script is undoubtedly syllabic, as in the Linear B Greek inscriptions of Crete, Pylos, and Mycenae.

(3) If the number of characters ranges in the hundreds or thousands, one may safely assume an ideotypic writing system, as for Modern Chinese.

The first goal in the decipherment of a phonotypic system must be the assignment of correct phonological values to the characters. Then, if one knows (i.e., 'understands') either the language itself or a genetically related language or even a later version of the same language, one can assign meanings to the characters or sequences of characters, either directly or by means of comparison with the other languages.

In the assignment of phonological values, one has two major approaches both of which have been used with success either individually or together:

(1) The identification by one means or another of any given

word, from which comes the segmenting of the characters for the word in accordance with their distribution in the word

(2) A statistical count for relative frequency of characters and the assignment of values attached to the normal frequency distribution for the specific language

The example of Bauer's guess about the name of the implement on which recurring sets of characters appeared illustrates one approach to the identification of a word. Bauer suspected that the language in question was a Northwest Semitic dialect, and so he noted that the Hebrew word for 'axe' also was (and is) normally written with four characters whose phonological values are /grzn/. In addition, he noted that certain sequences of three sets of characters, which he took to be the names of the owners of the axes, had a middle word whose last symbol was the same as the final symbol of the word for 'axe.' Since a common Semitic practice was to call someone "X son of Y" and since the word for 'son' appears in Hebrew as *bn* and in Arabic as *ibn,* he had a confirmation of the symbol for *n.* Referring back, he was able to assign the value of /b/ to the first symbol of the word for 'son.' In actual fact, it took Bauer only a few weeks to decipher the writing system once the first texts became available to him. Furthermore two other scholars, E. Dhorme and Ch. Virolleaud, accomplished the same feat, independently. The accuracy of their decipherments was later confirmed in a variety of ways, one, for instance, being a list of names of deities appearing in some of the longer texts that contained mythological material. Given the phonological values assigned, the names of these deities turned out to be identical with the deities known by the Hurrians. Furthermore the texts themselves made excellent sense, displaying vocabulary and grammar similar to that of other Semitic languages, particularly those of the Canaanite branch of Northwest Semitic. (This branch includes Hebrew, Phoenician, and Moabite. See the chart in Sec. 10.) The major assumption made by Bauer and the others was that this language was Semitic, a fortunate guess.

Most often in decipherments the main way of identifying some word of known pronunciation, whence phonological values can be assigned to characters, is the recognition of one or more proper names—either of individuals, normally kings or gods, or of places. With the Egyptian hieroglyphics, Champollion recognized two names as those of Ptolemy and Cleopatra, both of them appearing in cartouches (rounded frames used in outlining the names of gods and royalty). Since a lion appeared in second position for the latter name and in fourth position for the former, he assigned it the value of /l/. In a similar fashion, since a /p/ appears in both names, and a square symbol occurred in the position in each, he knew he was on the right track. One symbol, that of a bird, repeated itself in the name of *Cleopatra,* hence he assigned it an /a/ value, inasmuch as /a/ was the only phoneme that occurred twice in that name. Then, filling in both backwards and forwards, he arrived at phonological values for the other characters.

The decipherment of Old Persian, first presented by Georg Friedrich Grotefend to the Learned Society of Göttingen on September 4, 1802, rested on two major premises plus some good detective work. He correctly assumed, for reasons which need not concern us here, (a) that certain inscriptions were written in Old Persian by kings of the Achaemenides family, and (b) that the cuneiform writing itself was alphabetic rather than syllabic or ideographic. He arrived at the latter conclusion, not by counting all of the characters found (thirty-nine), a procedure which would have given him the same information, but by counting the number of characters occurring between diagonal wedges which had already been identified by others as possible word-dividers. Since up to ten characters appeared between the wedges, he reasoned that few words if any could have ten syllables.

Grotefend then looked for recurring elements in the inscription, hoping to find the names of kings, together with their titles and parentage, a common formulaic pattern in antiquity. He did find one word repeated three times, character by character, and what looked like a fourth time but with an additional character at the end. He assumed that the word meant 'king' and that the expanded version might mean 'of kings,' whence the title "King, King of Kings, King. . . ." Additional material preceded and followed. In a second inscription he found the same "King, King of Kings" plus the word which preceded the titles of the first inscription. He guessed that he was dealing with a dynastic sequence in which father and son were mentioned. A third inscription yielded the word which had preceded the title of inscription two—a sequence of son, father, and grandfather, which may be expressed as A son of B, B son of C, and C. . . . The third inscription lacked the "King." He reasoned that not only did he have a sequence of three generations but that the grandfather had not been a king. The rest of his problem was partly genealogical, partly linguistic. On the basis of genealogies of the Persian kings, given by Herodotus, he settled on the sequence *Hytaspes, Darius,* and *Xerxes,* since Hytaspes, father of Darius, had not been a king.

Grotefend was aided in his search by a comparison of the relative lengths of the presumed names and also by negative evidence such as the fact that the initial character of each name was different than that of the others—a fact that helped rule out *Cambyses* and *Cyrus* from consideration. Given the names, he checked their modern versions in Iran, reasoning that the Greek forms might not be as close to the originals. He then substituted the phonological values thus obtained for the characters, and the initial phase of the decipherment was over, although four out of his fifteen assigned values were somewhat wrong because of changes in the language from ancient to modern times. Following a similar line of reasoning Henry Rawlinson deciphered Old Persian on his own, basing his analysis also on inscriptions of Darius and Xerxes, but using those at Behistun and not the ones used by Grotefend.

In 1952 Michael Ventris also relied on proper names to provide the code-breaking key, but his guess rested on the ancient names of cities and towns of Crete, not on personal names. Ventris likewise had the writings of ancient authors to guide him for the names, notably Homer, who gave the list of places which sent military forces to Troy. By counting syllables and looking for recurrent symbols, Ventris was able to assign names to sets of symbols. In this instance, every single character did not have to be worked out independently. Based on an idea first pursued by Dr. Alice Kober of Brooklyn, New York, who died prior to the actual decipherment, Ventris had worked out a grid of symbols which set the stage for the assignment of values to others once any known values were identified.

That the Linear B script was syllabic had been recognized by Sir Arthur Evans who had found the first clay tablets containing this sort of writing in 1900. Kober had noted that many words appeared in three forms, later referred to as Kober's triplets, with the first set of two or three characters being identical in each, but with the last character being different. Because of the nature of a syllabic writing system, the last syllable of an *inflected* language would have to take this form since that syllable might contain the same consonant—part of the stem of the word—in each instance, but the additional inflectional morpheme would differ somewhat for each inflection. Consider, for example three declensional forms of the Latin word *amīcus:*

amīcus   amīcī   amīcō

To write this word syllabically, one would use one character for the *ā-* and another for the *-mī-* in each of the words, but the characters for *-cus, -cī,* and *-cō* would necessarily be different. Yet they would all contain the *c* as part of their syllabic value. Thus, although one might not know which consonant was included in each of the three, one would know that all three had the same consonant. If one should then identify any one of the three characters as containing this *c,* one would also know that the other two, likewise, contained it. By grouping all such "triplets" together in rows and columns, one would arrive at the sort of grid worked out by Ventris.

The accuracy of this grid (see Fig. 8) depended on the correct grouping of vowels as well as consonants. Yet given this structuring, as soon as Ventris had identified five characters, the values of more than thirty immediately appeared simply by projecting consonants across the triplet consonantal row, and the vowels down to vocalic groupings. Wherever an intersection of vowel and consonant occurred, Ventris had a syllabic value. Inserting the values arrived at first by his guess regarding place names, and then those ascertained by projection on the gird, Ventris was able to decipher many of the words on the tablets.

When he made the values of the characters known, a number of scholars in different parts of the world were not only able to translate the texts, but they found striking confirmation of the accuracy of the decipherment. The little pictographic symbols contained images of cooking vessels, horses, and other recognizable items. The words that appeared next to the pictures invariably

Fig. 8 SIMPLIFIED GRID OF TENTATIVE SYLLABIC VALUES

	Vowel 1	Vowel 2	Vowel 3	Vowel 4	Vowel 5
Consonant 1					
Consonant 2					
Consonant 3					
Consonant 4					
Consonant 5					
Consonant 6					
Consonant 7					
Consonant 8					
Consonant 9					
Consonant 10					
Consonant 11					

represented the Greek words for these items: *ti-ri-po-de* 'tripod,' for the three-footed pot, *ti-ri-o-we* for a 'three-handled pot,' *qe-to-ro-we* for a 'fourhandled pot,' and so on. Even after he had achieved the decipherment Ventris was not sure he was correct because the Greek of the tablets was unlike that which he had learned as a student: it was far older. Many of the sound changes such as that of Indo-European /kʷ/ to /p/, /t/, or /k/, depending on position, had not yet taken place. Thus the word for horse, *hippos* in Classical Greek, appeared as *i-qo* in Linear B, preserving a form similar to that seen in the Latin *equus* 'horse.' Professional linguists—Ventris was an architect—immediately recognized the accuracy of the de-

Fig. 9 THE SAME GRID (VALUES INSERTED)

	a	e	i	o	u
p–	/pa/	/pe/	/pi/	/po/	/pu/
t–	/ta/	/te/	/ti/	/to/	/tu/
k–	/ka/	/ke/	/ki/	/ko/	ku
d–	/da/	/de/	/di/	/do/	/du/
m–	/ma/	/me/	/mi/	/mo/	/mu/
n–	/na/	/ne/	/ni/	/no/	/nu/
r–	/ra/	/re/	/ri/	/ro/	/ru/
s–	/sa/	/se/	/si/	/so/	/su/
w–	/wa/	/we/	/wi/	/wo/	/wu/
y–	/ya/	/ye/		/yo/	/yu/
Zero	/a/	/e/	/i/	/o/	/u/

Note: 1. In the bottom row, one has pure vowels. The consonantal value is zero.

cipherment which showed exactly the forms one would reconstruct for the period 1450-1250 B.C.

If the language of the text is a known one and if this language

has been identified, one can decipher the text without any preliminary identification of words to serve as a guide to the phonological
values of the characters. A straight frequency count of the norm
that would occur in any sizable text if that text were written in the
appropriate type of script can provide the key. One need only count
the characters of the text in order of descending frequency and
then assign the phonological values—or even conceptual value if
one is counting ideotypic characters—in accord with this frequency
distribution. The greater the amount of the textual material, the
greater the accuracy of the match of the values. Indeed, if one
could reduce all known languages to a straight frequency count of
this type—according to each possibility—one could allow a com-
puter to run through all of the possibilities of the text, trying first
one language then another, until a set of values that made sense
were reached, provided only that the unknown script depicted one
of the four thousand or more languages now known or else some
language genetically related to any one of these.

8. LINGUISTIC-NONLINGUISTIC RELATIONSHIPS:
The Long-range Impact of Nonlinguistic Events on Language

Language is in a constant process of change. Even if there were no external influence on language, it would still change since there are internal pressures causing an evolution toward efficiency. However, since a language is not merely a single system, but rather a system of microsystems, each microsystem itself evolves toward the greatest possible efficiency. The details of what constitutes linguistic efficiency would take us far afield and will not concern us here. Nevertheless, one may note that when any feature in a microsystem changes in this structural evolution toward efficiency, it upsets the stability of some other system, which then initiates change geared to the attainment of the most efficient structure. Each change acts as the catalyst for another, in a never-ending chain reaction. Since language mirrors the culture in which it exists and which it signals, exolinguistic or nonlinguistic change also can cause a chain reaction within the linguistic system. The extent to which this reaction reflects the external events and the long-term continuance of a chain reaction is rarely understood. It may be desirable therefore to consider how far a single nonlinguistic event can bring about linguistic restructuring.

Latin, a subbranch of the Latin-Faliscan division of Italic, an Indo-European language, followed the rest of the Indo-European languages in contrasting singular and plural forms of the second person of the personal pronouns. Thus, one had *tū* 'you, singular' versus *vōs* 'you, plural,' the former being used when addressing one person, and the latter, when addressing more than one. This was the pattern that prevailed throughout Indo-European, with the exception of those few languages which still preserved an old dual category (later lost in all branches of the family), that once had been used in addressing just two people.

In Rome, a magistrate when sitting in his official public capacity, represented all of the people of the country, not just himself. Accordingly he was addressed by the plural form, *vōs*, not by *tū*, as he might have been had he been acting in his capacity as a private citizen. The magistrate, on the other hand, when speaking to a plaintiff or to the plaintiff's advocate would use *tū* to address the private citizen, as a single individual. Thus, all day long he was addressed as *vōs* and he, in turn, addressed all others as *tū*. Of course, on occasion, a lawyer might address the magistrate after court hours, but, having used *vōs* so frequently in court, he was unlikely to switch abruptly to the now correct *tū* form.

Although in principle anyone could rise to be a magistrate as long as he had never been a slave, the actual situation was quite different at that period. Virtually all Roman public offices were filled from a limited number of families with the proper political, social, and financial connections. Since, also, once a man had held a particular office, he was accorded an honorific associated with that office for the rest of his life—i.e., a former consul was ever after referred to as *consulāris*, 'a consular man' or 'a man who has borne the rank of consul'—a magistrate was virtually entitled to proper deference even when he no longer held office, let alone when he was acting in his private rather than public capacity. Thus the dichotomy between a singular versus plural function-marking subtly and slowly shifted to one which marked social class since, *de facto*, with rare exceptions, only the "upper" classes ever held the higher public offices. The only people never to address the official in the plural were the members of his immediate family and close friends, since they normally never encountered him in his role as representative of the populace. To them he was only a single person, hence their use of *tū*. This use (except by intimates), of *tū* versus *vōs* as a class rather than a number mark, descended into the Romance languages which eventually evolved out of Latin.

With the Norman Conquest in 1066, French became the language spoken by the nobility of England and by the higher echelons of the ecclesiastical hierarchy, since with few exceptions the Normans replaced the incumbents with their own supporters, all speakers of Norman French. For far more than a century and a half this linguistically strange situation prevailed in England, with the upper classes, both civil and church, speaking French, and the lower classes speaking English (actually Middle English).

In Old English (449 to about 1050 or 1100) the pronouns *þū, þīn, þē, þec* ('you, singular' in the nominative, genitive, dative, and accusative cases) and *gē, ēower, ēow, ēowic* ('you, plural' in the same cases) contrasted singular versus plural forms as had the very old Latin at one time. The French used the pronominal dichotomy as a mark of social standing. Outside of the intimate family group where the dichotomy did not apply, one addressed an inferior with *tu* and a superior with *vous* (the descendant of the Latin *vōs*). Aside from a limited amount of lexical borrowing in particular areas, the two languages, although coexisting in the same territory had little impact on each other until the thirteenth century.

In 1204 King John of England married Isabel d'Angoulême, who happened also to have been engaged to Hugh de Lusignan, a member of a powerful and influential French family. Since he anticipated trouble anyway, John took the initiative and attacked the Lusignans. The latter complained to the French king, who promptly ordered John—in John's capacity as Duke of Normandy, which post made him a theoretical vassal of the French throne—to come to Paris for judgment. When the English king prudently refused, the French drove the English from Normandy. This act was the starting point for the loss of the "English" possessions in France—most of the English nobility, actually of Norman lineage, having owned property on both sides of the Channel.

The Norman English nobility lost their remaining foothold in France in 1244 when the French king, becoming aware of the danger of allowing many of his nobles to have divided loyalties—to him as the French king because of their French possessions and also to the English king because of their English possessions—decreed that these individuals could keep either their properties in England or those in France, but not both. Those who chose to be English were thus cut off from their customary practice of spending all or most of the year in France. Being forced to remain in England and being surrounded by English speakers, they then started to use the language of the land they ruled. In so doing, they caused many thousands of French loan words to enter English: whenever they couldn't think of the English word, they used the French. An abrupt rise in French loan words took place starting around 1250, shortly after the French decree. Besides the lexical additions, the French class-marking use of the personal pronouns was engrafted upon English where it might have remained indefinitely were it not for a historical event that took place approximately a century later.

In the year 1348, the bubonic plague, or Black Death, which had swept across the European continent, finally reached England. According to various estimates, it wiped out from thirty to sixty per cent of the population, as it had elsewhere. The nobles, of course, having a freedom of movement denied to the peasants, were able to get away from the path of the greatest contagion. The lower classes, however, were hit harder than the upper classes and in consequence, able-bodied workers came to be in short supply. The middle classes, too, dwelling in the more crowded cities were reduced in numbers. With the working classes thus affected, they were in a position to demand and receive greater respect from the nobility. Various historical events such as the Peasants' Revolt of 1381 attest the social restructuring coming about immediately after the Plague. This restructuring was to set in motion a chain reaction in the language—a reaction which is still causing linguistic repercussions to this very day.

The first result of the demand for greater respect was the lessened frequency of the *thou, thine, thee* forms among the groups that had adopted the French-based social dichotomy of the pronouns. Although some groups such as the Quakers had maintained the original singular versus plural dichotomy, in general, the social-marking function had prevailed. Thus the *ye, your,* and *you* forms, which had evolved from the earlier *gē, ēower,* and *ēow* of Old English, gradually replaced the once contrastive set. Of the group extending its domain, eventually the *ye* and *you* subject-versus-object-marking forms merged, leaving only *you* and *your,* with no singular-versus-plural contrast in the second person parallel to that for the first and third persons (i.e., *I* versus *we* or *he* versus *they*) or for most nouns (*chair* versus *chairs, book* versus *books,* etc.).

Now Middle English (1050-1450) had a fuller set of verbal endings than is seen in Modern English:

	SINGULAR	PLURAL
FIRST PERSON	-e	-eth, -s, or -en
		(these forms used
SECOND PERSON	-est	throughout the plural,
		the particular form
THIRD PERSON	-eth or -s	depending on the
		specific dialect)

The -est verbal ending had regularly appeared with the thou second-person-singular form, later the inferiority marker. With the declining use of thou came the parallel loss of this -est verbal ending. When ye (later you) came into greater use, it took the corresponding verbal form that correlated with it, -eth in some dialects, -s in others, and -en in those which were eventually to become the standard pattern (with the later loss of -eth and -s). Thus the Plague resulted in two changes, not just one, in the fourteenth century. Yet these two changes had a profound impact on the rest of the structure.

In the course of Middle English—earlier in some dialects, later in others—final n ultimately disappeared, perhaps around 1250 to 1300. At the end of the Middle English period, word-final -e (pronounced /ə/, the final vowel of Cuba) disappeared. Thus the Middle English verbal pattern came to have the following shape in the Early Modern period:

	SINGULAR	PLURAL
FIRST PERSON	-	-
SECOND PERSON	-	-
THIRD PERSON	-eth or -s	-

In other words, the loss of the second-person singular (inferior) -eth,

coupled with the normal results of two phonological changes motivated by internal structural reasons, brought about a pattern in
which only the third-person singular was marked. Both third-person
marks occurred down through Shakespeare's time in free distribution: "The quality of mercy . . . bless*eth* him that give*s* and him that
receive*s*." Shortly thereafter the *-eth* variant disappeared from
standard speech leaving only the sibilant morpheme as the sole
mark of person or number.

Now linguistic evolution is efficiency-directed, although the
nature of the efficiency may vary. One type of efficiency eliminates
redundancy: language tends to keep a one-to-one balance between
function and the means of manifesting that function. This variety
led to disuse of the *-eth* in favor of the *-s*. Here there were two
marks for a single function, and one represented a redundancy,
hence its elimination. Another type of efficiency rests on the degree
of integration that a feature has within a system. Here, since person
was being marked in the verb only in the third person of the singular of some verbs (note that the model auxiliaries such as *can, may,
will,* or *shall* lack the characteristic *-s*, as in *jumps*) and then only in
the present (the past tense, as *jumped,* lacks the *-s*), there exists a
structural pressure to eliminate this *-s* and generally to avoid marking person and number at all in the verb. This pressure has already
caused some dialects still regarded as substandard to drop the *-s*,
although the patterns used by well educated individuals still keep it.
Yet even here there are signs of an incipient loss, particularly when
the phonological environment favors it. The negative of *He does*
should be *He does not* or, more informally, *He doesn't.* In recent
decades even some who are relatively well educated have been sub-
stituting *He don't* though they still retain *He does not* in the un-
contracted variant. This usage has been creeping up the scale of
acceptability although virtually all language purists insist that *He
doesn't* is the only permissible contraction. This author—a linguist
used to recording what he hears—has occasionally observed college
English teachers, including one department chairman, employing
He don't in animated and informal discourse. Needless to say, the
professors would deny this fact since it goes against their professional ethos to allow linguistic evolution, even when structurally
motivated.

The verb *be* still preserves three separate forms in the present —*am, are* and *is*—and two in the past—*was* and *were*. Yet the loss of support for the marking of number and person in the present of the verb has caused the generalization of one or another of the *be* forms for all persons and both numbers:

I is	*We is*
You is	*You is*
He is	*They is*
I am	*We am*
You am	*You am*
He am	*They am*

This generalization to be sure has taken place only in a few patterns, those usually described as substandard or uneducated, but the pressure toward the pattern is still operative. Thus a popular song of a few decades ago has the line, "Is you is or is you ain't my baby?" Grandpa McCoy on a recent television program used to say, "We is what we is."

The pronominal pattern which emerged as the result of the Plague was the following:

	SINGULAR	PLURAL
FIRST PERSON	*I*	*we*
SECOND PERSON	*you*	*you*
THIRD PERSON	*he, she, it*	*they*

As can be seen, there is no overt differentiation between second-person forms of the singular and plural. Yet this number-marking function is well embedded in the language: other parts of the pronominal pattern have it, as in *I* versus *we* or *he, she,* or *it* versus *they;* nouns have it, as in *chair* versus *chairs;* demonstratives have it, as in *this* versus *these* or *that* versus *those;* even some adjectives mark number, though not dichotomously (e.g., *both,* which is plural). Since number is so well integrated into the system, here the pressure is in the direction of the restoration of a formal, distinct marking of the function. The statistically predominant mark of plurality is the sibilant, as seen in *boys* or *chairs*. On the model of *boys* to *boys* one gets a *you* to what? The answer, of course is *youse,* a form that *has* evolved. Since this form has appeared first among the uneducated, it has come to be associated with one's lack of education, whence its avoidance in the prestige dialects. Nevertheless the pressure for the marking of plurality remains, giving rise to various other innovations—*you uns, you all,* Jamaican Creole *unu,* and so on.

Thus one sees a still operative restructuring which represents the resultant of the chain reaction initiated by the bubonic plague of the fourteenth century. One may perhaps note the irony in the following: a restructuring of society caused the demand for greater respect, whence arose the loss of one pronoun and one verbal ending. The consequences of these changes in combination with others which were motivated by other pressures caused the evolution of new forms. Finally, those who use these structure-motivated forms are categorized as belonging to a class which receives less respect because of this use. Eventually, however, the innovations will extend their domain and even the prestige groups will employ both these forms and others which are still developing.

9 LINGUISTIC SYSTEMS AS
ANALYTICAL MODELS

As repeatedly asserted, language is a system of systems—phonological systems, grammatical systems, semantic systems, and so on—each with its own internal structuring subject to general laws, some of which are just beginning to be understood, others long recognized but still not fully comprehended in any satisfactory way. Language, of course, is part of the entire sociocultural system and therefore reflects by way of appropriate mechanisms the cognitive scheme of that system. This fact served as the basis—and justification—for Section 5, which dealt with sociocultural reconstruction. The internal dynamics of languages represent finely attuned balances between the cognitive needs of the members of the culture, both in respect to communication and thinking, and general (evolutionary?) principles, such as those dictated by efficiency needs.

It is not the intent of this book to bring nonlinguists to the frontiers of linguistic research but rather to provide them with practical procedures useful for their own disciplines. Nevertheless a couple of simple examples may serve to indicate at least some of the analytic potentialities even for the other social sciences once linguists have solved certain of their own problems. Needless to say, the reverse holds true as well. However, in a number of ways linguistic data are more readily analyzed or analyzable than nonlinguistic data, so the linguistic theorist may sometimes be in an advantageous position to identify and elucidate his own and his colleagues' mutual concerns. Earlier sections of this book have shown how linguistic methodology can uncover fundamental information of diverse sorts regarding the sociocultural systems and their members. Linguistics as a developing science, however, may provide another kind of insight in addition to the foregoing: it may serve as a theoretical model for the understanding of the sociocultural mechanisms themselves, beyond the simple disclosure of the content and organization of the systems and facts related thereto.

The following sections offer two representative examples of the possible discovery of the *operative principles* of sociocultural systems by means of linguistic models. The first one, that of the "rank-size law," was first observed and described by linguists, but its applications clearly go far beyond communicational phenomena. The principle would appear to have its roots in sociocultural systems generally. Neither the linguists who discovered the law nor the statisticians, demographers, economists, and others who later studied it know precisely why it works, but, within the limits mapped out in Section 9.1 the operative principle does seem to hold true. Section 9.2, on the other hand, illustrates a linguistic/non-linguistic analogue of another kind, namely that of the Verner's Law type. This phenomenon is better understood than the former, however; hence it may prove more useful as an analytic tool.

9.1 The Rank-size Law

One phenomenon generally applicable to the social sciences, but first recognized in its linguistic manifestation, is now sometimes described as "the rank-size law." It represents a statistical regularity, still not well understood, which apparently holds true in a number of diverse areas, including the linguistic. Put in its most abstract formulation, it asserts that, given quantifiable elements—e.g., numbers of words in a text, numbers of people in different cities, and so on—the absolute numbers of the different elements will bear, to a very close approximation, a consistent ratio expressed by the inverse of their frequency ranking in the group as a whole.

A simple illustration will clarify this statement. If all the words of a text are tabulated for frequency of occurrence, and if the word appearing most often is ranked as number 1, that appearing next most frequently is ranked as number 2, and so forth, the *actual* number of times that any two words appear will be inversely proportional to their relative frequency rankings. The first most frequent word will appear twice as often as the second (i.e., 2 to 1) and three times as often as the third (3 to 1), while the third will appear three times as often as the ninth (9 to 3) but only one and one-third times as often as the fourth (4 to 3). Thus if the word ranking number 1 should appear 100 times, one would find that the word ranking number 4 would appear 25 times. Why this phenomenon is so remains unknown, but a simple count of any linguistic text—even of this page—will reveal the principle at work. Furthermore the nature of the text seems to be irrelevant to the statistical phenomenon. The data may be taken from a novel, a letter, or a poem, from an ancient text or a modern one, from English or from Swahili. The source doesn't matter.

Of greater interest to theoreticians is the universality of the principle. If cities, for instance, are ranked by population, the absolute size of the populations of any two cities will maintain the same inverse proportion. For instance in 1960 Philadelphia, then the fourth most populous city with a count of 2,002,512 residents, had approximately three times (12-to-4) the population of San Francisco, whose 740,026 people caused it to be ranked twelfth. Minor details fluctuate, perhaps subject to principles or conditions not yet identified, but the regularity of the principle is striking.

9.2 A Sociocultural Analogue of Verner's Law

The analysis of linguistic systems reveals that both the potentialities and the directions for change lie in the structure of a system. Certain systems are stable; others, unstable. All unstable systems tend to evolve by very precise routes toward stability.

Early linguists used to look at the accidental and irrelevant properties of the linguistic systems which they chanced to analyze. They failed to grasp the generalized nature of particular structural relationships which could be embodied in different systems at different times or in different places. Not having examined a variety of data, they never understood that absolutely every time certain structures occurred the range of developments was very narrowly delimited. Grimm's Law, for example, originally formulated back in 1822, represented a first step—but only a first step—toward a type of structural thinking. Grimm recognized that specific shifts from Indo-European to Germanic showed a certain parallelism. Hence he formulated his observations in his statement of three *sets* of changes (listed in Sec. 4.11). His insight was an important one, but it lacked the further perspective (*a*) that the Germanic changes represented the start toward a subtractive solution of a phonological structural instability but with abortive feedback from the morphological level which precluded the completion of this maneuver, (*b*) that the Germanic developments represented only one out of many possible reactions toward one instability of the Indo-European system of stops, and, of greatest consequence here, (*c*) that the particular features underlying the system—here voicing or its lack and aspiration or its lack—were of less relevance than the actual realizations of combinations of those or of other features. Phenomena similar to the Grimm's law developments take place in systems organized around completely different features, provided that the structural combinations are the same.

Section 4 showed how a phoneme represents the realization of a bundle of co-occurring distinctive articulatory features. Thus the phoneme /d/ represents (*a*) complete closure rather than incomplete closure, (*b*) oral rather than nasal articulation, (*c*) an alveolar rather than a nonalveolar point of contact, and (*d*) a voiced rather than an unvoiced manipulation. It involves a complex of many simultaneously or (relatively simultaneously) realized features. In a like manner, any word represents the manifestation of a complete bundle of *semantic* parameters. In fact every discrete category at every level represents a nexus of interrelationships. Every relationship rests on a functional contrast. For instance, for voicing of the /d/ to be relevant to the system, that system had to have an unvoiced counterpart (or set of counterparts) to the voiced member(s), as in /t/. For nonnasality to be relevant there had to be nasal contrasts, as in /n/ which differs from the /d/ only by the nonclosure of the opening into the nasal chamber. In a similar fashion singularity is relevant for verbs precisely because plurality is a potential contrast. Without the possible choice of plurality, singularity would not play the same role in the system. The category "verb" can be (and has been) described as the simultaneous realization of verbal parameters such as number, tense, and aspect.

It is perhaps, not exactly customary to compare human beings to phonemes or to other linguistic entities, yet in some ways a human being is the same as all other human beings while he is simultaneously different from every other person. Analytically he may be defined by his shared and differentiating parameters. Thus he is a father as opposed to a non-father, an Episcopalian as opposed to a non-Episcopalian, an accountant as opposed to a non-accountant, and so on. Every relevant parameter will dictate certain probabilities about his functioning in the human system. The fact that he is an accountant, for example, means that he will normally operate at specific fixed times with pencil and paper rather than with thermometer and stethoscope or monkey wrench or hammer. His being an accountant would not, of course, preclude his using a thermometer on rare occasions (e.g., if his child were sick), but such use would not be in his function as accountant. It might perhaps be a reflex of his being a father (another of the parameters which define him). He might likewise use a wrench, but again not in his capacity as an accountant. Such use might arise if he owned a car—another parameter—which would group him together with all other car owners and apart from all nonowners.

Linguistic phenomena such as those encompassed under "Grimm's Law," reveal this central fact about systemic dynamics: individual entities of a system do not normally change *as individual entities;* they change in sets according to their shared and differentiating parameters. The pattern itself as defined by the underlying parameters of its constituents dictates the possible directions for change. For example, Grimm's Law codifies the changes undergone by an entire set of stop consonants from Indo-European to Germanic. There were nonstops, such as fricatives, in the Indo-European consonantal pattern, but they never partook of the changes since they were not integrated into the pattern by virtue of shared parameters. When Grimm's Law chain reaction caused the voiceless stops to become nonstops, however, the s which previously had existed as an entity outside this microsystem now became integrated with this new set of voiceless fricatives—ϕ, θ, χ, and χ^w—by reason of its sharing the two parameters, voicelessness and fricative articulation with the other phonemes. Consequently it participated thereafter in all changes undergone by other members of its own set-class. When, under conditions formulated by the Danish scholar Karl Verner, the other voiceless fricatives became voiced, so did the *s* (which thus became *z*). When some of these now voiced fricatives became voiced stops (by making a complete and firm closure rather than an incomplete or lax one at the point of articulation), the *z* (earlier *s*) likewise became a voiced stop—originally an iterative stop (i.e., a trill, to differentiate it from the resultant of another fricative's loss of closure), later an *r*. The details perhaps are of greater concern to the professional linguist than to the historian, but the dynamics of the Grimm's Law/Verner's Law complex should not be, since they underlie not only other linguistic phenomena but also may account for some nonlinguistic sociocultural developments as well. Consider, for instance, an analogue of the foregoing development.

In the middle ages all formal teaching in Europe was done by priests, who were always priests first and teachers second. They were subject to the absolute rule of the Church and no dissent was even thinkable let alone permissible. No priest would ever have considered going on strike at that time. The consequences would have been disastrous to him to say the least. Later, however, with the Renaissance there arose secular schools not connected with the Church. With the advent of nonecclesiastic schools came the emergence of nonecclesiastic teachers. Yet from the point of view of systemic dynamics the rise of the latter class necessarily relates to the structuring of the teaching priests in the macrosystem. By virtue of the existence of the secular teachers, the teaching priests were now subject to two sharply defined and potentially conflicting parameters. Previously they had been priests, subject to ecclesiastic pressures. No nonecclesiastical pressures pertained to them any more than such pressures did to any priests. Now, however, the teaching priests belonged to two set-classes: (*a*) priests, who were, as such, subject to ecclesiastical pressures, and (*b*) educators, who were, as such, subject to the same educational pressures which pertain to other educators. When, through various restructurings (that need not concern us here), teachers started to go on strike for better wages or better working conditions, *it was implicit in the system* that the teaching priests would also do so. It was not simply an accident of history. Furthermore, the precision of statement that characterizes the modern versions of the Grimm's Law/Verner's Law complex is not the same as an anecdotal recasting of some imperfectly understood developments. It poses problems of predictability and scientific explanation. The foregoing example by itself does not, of course, constitute compelling proof. It should, however, reopen certain basic questions. Aside from the labels of the parameters, the structuring of the phonological example and that of the teaching priests are the same.

10. LANGUAGE CLASSIFICATION

10.1 The Basis of Classification

Linguists generally classify language in accordance with any one of three major criteria:

(1) Geographical distribution
(2) Genetic relationship
(3) Typological structure

10.11 Geographical Distribution

The first basis, that which rests on geographical distribution, states merely where a language is or was spoken. For example, the first English settlers in the New World lumped all Amerindian languages together as "Indian," even though some of these were unrelated to each other. One may speak of "African" languages, disregarding genetic or other relationships, similarities, or dissimilarities. Normally this classificational scheme is a first-stage analysis, useful where no other information is known.

10.12 Genetic Relationship

The second classificational criterion is that of genetic relationship. Once languages can be shown to have descended from some single ancestral source, perhaps (though not necessarily) no longer attested, they may be grouped together. Normally genetic statements take the form of branching-tree diagrams indicating subgroupings of nearer or more distant relationships as in the following:

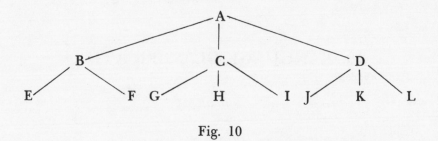

Fig. 10

This diagram sets up Language A as the ancestor of the others, and asserts that A split into B, C, and D. It states further that B later split into E and F; C, into G, H, and I; and D, into J, K, and L. In essence, it is also a statement that E is more closely related to F than K or L, historically speaking.

Although genetic statements hold historical implications, they may rest on purely synchronic evidence. Thus, even if B, C, and D had all disappeared, as well as A (their hypothetical ancestor), one could still reconstruct the intermediate stages on the basis of the information available in E, F, G, H, I, J, K, and L. Both the assertion of the gross genetic relationship and the refinement of the details would depend on the identification of systematic equations at each level, but most importantly at the phonological. The breakdown into subbranches would rest on shared versus differentiated features. It is possible, of course, for two languages to undergo some of the same changes once the speakers of the languages have separated, but it grows statistically less and less probable that they will share any constellation of innovations (which may be additions to, modifications of, or deletions of parts of the original pattern). Every different independent development is evidence for a split. Those languages which share the greater number of innovations are presumably those which remained together the longest before their divergence.

Many linguists would rate morphological similarity as next in importance to phonology in setting up genetic relationships. The point is a debatable one although it carries greater weight in assessing close rather than very remote relationships. Each phonological change begets primary morphological change. Yet, since some morphological changes beget other morphological mutations, the evolution becomes geometrically not arithmetically progressive at the morphological level. In the identification of very distant genetic connections, it well may be that the conceptual functions and categories of the language are most reliable and resistant to change, and, therefore, may preserve for a longer period parts of the inherited pattern lost or redistributed in the manifesting systems. An example may clarify the point.

In Indo-European the object (or "accusative") function was signified by the addition of an -*m* to the stem of the substantive. This -*m* was appended to any stem regardless of what phoneme it ended with. Thus an *o*-stem word would have *-*om*, a *u*-stem, *-*um*, and so forth. In the evolution from Proto-Indo-European down to the attested languages, each subgroup's phonological system evolved, whence its morphological and other systems likewise changed. Since Indo-European *o* became *a* in the Indo-Iranian subgroup, the accusative ending of Indo-European *o*-stems became -*am* (from earlier *-*om*). In Greek, the final -*m* of Indo-European developed to -*n*, hence -*on* as the accusative of *o*-stems (from the same earlier *-*om* of Indo-European). In Latin *-*om* evolved to -*um*. In each of these three language groups the relationship of the accusative singular— -*am, on*, or -*um* respectively—remained transparently as the anticipated resultant of the same earlier *-*om*, whereby this set of morphological facts supports a genetic hypothesis. On the other hand, in the evolution to Germanic and eventually to English, the *-*om* did not simply change: it disappeared completely. Old English, of course, did not simply drop the marking of the functional category; it merely switched to word order to do the same job. The function itself remained in the language. Thus *John hit Peter* and *Peter hit John* are different statements since the specification of subject and object rests in the relevant order. Not all languages, however, mark subject or object relationships. Hence a grouping of all languages by functional categories might disclose that those languages with the same categories evince some genetic connections with each other even though the particular devices used to mark the functions have diverged greatly in the millennia of separation.

10.13 Typological Structure

Languages, whether genetically related or not, whether spoken in the same area or not, may resemble each other, and thus may be classified together on the basis of some part or parts of their structure. The major subclasses would rest on the comparison of conceptual structures, manifesting structures, or both.

As suggested, since the conceptual functions resist loss, provided they are well integrated in the sociocultural macrosystem, merely shifting from one level to another the particular manner of marking the function, conceptual typologizing of languages may disclose remote genetic relationships. Nonetheless, many scholars would assert a more basic use for a conceptual typology. Such a classification would indicate the similarity or dissimilarity of cultures and of the ways in which their members view the world. In a manner of speaking, such an analysis would measure a compatibility quotient. For example, it has been reported that in one cultural system of the Northern Belgian Congo the natives have absolutely no words for color since hue plays no role at all in their lives. They never color their clothing nor bodies nor dwellings as do the natives of other cultures—including our own. Their garb consists of cloth made of plain bark, treated for softness, but not for chromatic appeal. No pictures adorn their walls, and so forth. In this respect the achromatic culture differs greatly from most of Western European civilization, where more than a million dollars may be paid for a single painting, and where women spend, quite literally, billions of dollars for lipstick, rouge, eye shadow, nail polish, and other cosmetics. It has been shown that the average student in a New York City college can within a very short time, think of close to thirty words just for the color red (e.g., *scarlet, alizarine, cerise, crimson*).

The fact that not all European languages have the wealth of synonyms that English has in this particular conceptual field is perhaps less relevant than the existence of well-developed lexicons dealing with color—a reflex of a world view more notable to English speakers by a total lack than by some internal differentiation. If an English-speaking woman were to dress in bark cloth, she would undoubtedly—unlike the Congo woman—be critically aware of the browns or tans of the bark and would select her accessories to match. The Congo woman might very well choose the same items, but the choices would rest on something other than color, a feature so remote from the consideration of the Congo culture that it is not rejected: it does not even rise to the level of awareness necessary for rejection.

A sophisticated conceptual analysis might properly quantify the degree of differentiation within a field (e.g., how many words are there for a given color or how many subdivisions of the concept of warfare?). This breakdown would facilitate cross-cultural comparison. Another type of observation relevant to such a study would describe which conceptual categories have to be marked in a system. In the Indo-European languages, for instance, number and time and certain types of aspect (completive versus incompletive, progressive versus aprogressive, etc.) must be marked. In other linguistic systems they may be marked but need not be.

Thus far, no thoroughgoing, or even partial, concept-oriented typology has been advanced although the thrust of a number of major analytic orientations such as the tagmemic school or that of functional syntax makes such a project an eventual certainty. Such a typology had never been suggested, however, until 1960, at which time Professor André Martinet appended a few observations relevant to the subject to a trail-blazing article on functional syntax.

Typologizing on the basis of manifesting structures is more traditional in linguistics, although modern theorists now realize that manifesting structures evolve and change quite readily. August Schleicher, a nineteenth century German philologist, much influenced by Hegel and with the latter's ideas of thesis, antithesis, and synthesis, was the first to attempt a form-based typology, taking over certain observations of the Danish linguist Rasmus Rask, a pioneer in the analysis of Indo-European morphology. It would be misleading as well as unfair—after all, over a century has passed since Schleicher's death (1868)—to restate his theory, but the following practical application (not possible at all in his era) may clarify the nature of the scheme.

One may hypothesize on the basis of internal evidence a stage of Indo-European in which each function was marked by a single morpheme. Perhaps the sequence of morphemes was irrelevant then. This period may be called *analytic,* with a one-morpheme-to-one-function marking system. Eventually certain morphemes started to occur so frequently—say the marking of the pronoun subject plus the once-separate verbal-notion—that these clusters of morphemes started to be "felt" as constituent entities of "words." Prior to this time, in a sense, the different morphemes, which had been separable, were the words. Now, however, the words consisted of combinations of morphemes. As long as each element was recognizable, one may refer to this period as the *agglutinative* ('clumping together'). After the lapse of still more time, some of the morphemes which had been independent entities in stage 1 (the analytic), then constituents still analytically identifiable in stage 2, merged so thoroughly in the next phase that one could no longer separate the elements in such a way as to assign each unit its function. This phase may be labeled the *inflectional.* Thus, for instance, the ending *-ī* of Latin *hominī* 'to a man' marked two functional relationships: one was that of 'indirect object' (expressed by 'to' in the translation), and the other was that of singularity (one man, not two or more). There was no way of indicating which part of the *-ī* signified the 'indirect object' and which 'the singular.' Eventually the progress of change caused some of these inflectional endings to disappear, and the languages simply re-marked the functions—this time by separate words (e.g., Modern French *à un homme,* 'to a man'), a return to the earlier analytic pattern.

There are some minor additional complications depending on the hierarchal stage in the constituent structure at which position becomes inflexible (e.g., if the entire sentence is a single word or if some smaller segment is). This problem need not concern us. One may note however that no language at all is purely inflectional or purely polysynthetic (if the entire sentence is a word). One encounters mixed types, with some transparent bound-morphological marks, some fused, some free. Furthermore, this overlapping of constituent stages leads to problems regarding rules of agreement, whose violation causes either anomaly or ungrammaticality in a language. A central requirement of good communication is that no signal be ambiguous (unless deliberately so) or contradictory. Thus, in Indo-European the verbal act was performed by an actor signified by an affixed personal pronoun, as the *-ō* of Latin *ferō,* Greek *pʰerō,* or the *-u* of the Old English *beru* (Anglian dialects), all meaning 'I bear,' and all deriving the bound pronoun from one which had once been a separate word. In Latin and Greek no additional marking of 'I' was necessary, beyond the ending *-ō* (except for reasons of emphatic contrast—e.g., *'I* rather than *you').* In Old English and later in the Romance languages when the pronominal ending started to be lost in specific contexts, it became necessary once again to mark the 'I,' this time by the separate word 'I,' Old English *ic* or French *je* (both descended from the same Indo-European source, seen as *ego* in Latin). The occasional redundancy of marking which occurred when the earlier ending did not completely disappear made agreement of subject and verb a necessity. One could not use 'I' with a verbal form which still preserved a vestige of an old third-person ending (e.g., **I goes* or **I goeth)* or else there would have been a contradiction of signals.

The form-based typology sometimes facilitates genetic comparison, where the languages are related closely enough. Otherwise it probably has little interest for the historian.

10.2 A Survey of Some Major Genetic Classifications

The French Academy once computed the number of languages in the world as exactly two thousand seven hundred and ninety-six. Other studies put the number at well over four thousand. Many of these languages themselves subdivide into different, presumably mutually intelligible, divisions, commonly called "dialects," or "subsystems." Obviously no more than the most cursory survey may be included here since a full classification together with appropriate discussions concerning the bases for the classification would require many volumes, not just a brief chapter. This section outlines a few of the large genetically related groups, but makes no claims as to the completeness or accuracy of the listing. A brief consideration, say, of just the Austronesian family alone, which includes at least five hundred discrete languages spread across the Pacific and Indian Oceans and over a three thousand mile north-to-south range, will suggest why. It is highly likely that many as yet uncharted islands contain speakers of still other languages belonging to this large group. Clearly one cannot classify or list that which is not yet even known. Furthermore, any scholar interested in pursuing the complex interrelationships of the peoples speaking languages of one or another such group can readily be relied upon also to have the perspicuity to recognize probable genetic relationships provided he obtains samples of the languages in question.

THE INDO-EUROPEAN FAMILY

I. Celtic
    A. Goidelic (or Q-Celtic)
        1. Old Irish
        2. Manx
    B. Brythonic (or P-Celtic)
        1. Welsh
        2. Breton
        3. Cornish
II. Germanic
    A. West
        1. Low
            a. Old Saxon
            b. Old Low Franconian (Old Dutch)
            c. Old Frisian
            d. Old English
        2. High (= Old High German)
III. Italic
    A. Latino-Faliscan
        1. Latin
        2. Faliscan
    B. Osco-Umbrian
        1. Oscan
        2. Umbrian
    C. Sabellian
        1. Paelignian
        2. Marrucinian
        3. Vestinian

          4. Volscian
          5. Marsian
          6. Aeguian
          7. Sabine

IV. Greek

V. Albanian

VI. Illyrian

VII. Thraco-Phrygian
    A. Thracian
    B. Phrygian
    C. Armenian

VIII. Venetic

IX. Balto-Slavic
    A. Baltic
        1. Old Prussian
        2. Lithuanian
        3. Lettish (Latvian)
    B. Slavic
        1. Southern
            a. Old Church Slavic (Old Bulgarian)
            b. Serbo-Croatian
        2. Northern
            a. Great Russian (usually called simply Russian)
            b. White Russian
            c. Little Russian (also called Ukrainian or, in the older literature, Ruthenian)
        3. Western
            a. Polish
            b. Sorbo-Wendic
            c. Czecho-Slovak (also called Bohemian)

X. Indo-Iranian
    A. Indic
        1. Sanskrit
        2. Prakits
            a. Pali
            b. Magadhi
                (1) Bengali
                (2) Bihari

        (3) Assamese (not the Sino-Tibetan language which bears the same name)

        (4) Oriya

    c. Maharastri

        (1) Marathi

        (2) Sinhalese

    d. Sauraseni

        (1) Western Hindi

        (2) Panjabi

        (3) Sindhi

        (4) Gujarati

        (5) Rajasthani

        (6) Pahari

        (7) Bhili

        (8) Khandesi

    e. Paisaci

        (1) Pashai

        (2) Kafir

        (3) Khowar

        (4) Kasmiri

        (5) Kohistani

        (6) Shina

    f. Ardhamagadhi

        (1) Eastern Hindi

  B. Iranian

    1. Old Persian

    2. Avestan

XI. Tokharian

  A. Tokharian A

  B. Tokharian B

XII. Anatolian

  A. Cuneiform Hittite

  B. Hieroglyphic Hittite-Luvian

    1. Hieroglyphic Hittite

    2. Luvian

  C. Lycian

  D. Lydian (?)

THE URAL-ALTAIC FAMILY

I. Uralic (also called Fenno-Ugric)
  A. Finnish-Lapponic
    1. Finnish
    2. Lapponic
      a. Lapp
      b. Cheremis
      c. Mordvin
  B. Ugric
    1. Hungarian
    2. Ob-Ugrian
  C. Permian
  D. Samoyedic
II. Altaic
  A. Turkic
    1. Western
      a. Bashkir
      b. Chuvash
      c. Kirghiz
      d. Irtysh
    2. Central
      a. Chagatai
      b. Uzbeg
    3. Southern
      a. Azerbaidjani
      b. Turkoman
      c. Turkish (Osmanli or Ottoman)
      d. Balkan
      e. Kumic
    4. Eastern
      a. Altaic (proper)
      b. Telenget
  B. Mongol
    1. Eastern

        2. Northern
        3. Western
    C. Manchu-Tungus
        1. Manchu
        2. Tungus
           a. Oroch
           b. Kile
           c. Olcha (also called Mangun)
           d. Lamut
           e. Orochon
           f. Orog
           g. Yenesei Tungus
           h. Chapogir
           i. Shibä
    D. Japanese-Korean
        1. Japanese
        2. Korean

THE AFRO-ASIATIC (HAMITO-SEMITIC) FAMILY

  I. Egyptian (the language of the ancient hieroglyphs, which evolved to modern Coptic, not the Arabic now spoken in Egypt)
 II. Libyco-Berber
    A. Ancient Libyan
    B. Berber
        1. Southern
           a. Shluh
           b. Tuareg
           c. Zenaga
           d. Kabyl
        2. Northern
           a. Zenete
           b. Guanche (extinct; spoken in the Canary Islands until the seventeenth century A.D.)

III. Cushitic
- A. Northern
  1. Beja (Bedauye)
- B. Central
  1. Bogo (Bilin)
  2. Kamir
  3. Khamta
  4. Awiya
  5. Danot
  6. Kemant
  7. Kayla
  8. Quara
- C. Eastern
  1. Saho-Afar
     a. Saho
     b. Afar
  2. Somali
  3. Galla
  4. Konso
  5. Gelebra
  6. Marielle
  7. Gardula
  8. Gidole
  9. Gowaze
  10. Burji
  11. Sidamo
  12. Darasa
  13. Kambata
  14. Alaba
  15. Hayda
  16. Tambaro
- D. Western
  1. Janjero
  2. Wolano
  3. Zala
  4. Gofa
  5. Basketo

      6. Badito
      7. Haruro
      8. Zaysse
      9. Chara
    10. Gimira
    11. Benesho
    12. Nao
    13. Kaba
    14. Shako
    15. She
    16. Maji
    17. Kafa
    18. Garo
    19. Mocha
    20. Anfillo
    21. Shinasha
    22. Bako
    23. Amar
    24. Bana
    25. Dime
    26. Gayi
    27. Kerre
    28. Tsamai
    29. Doko
    30. Dollo
  E. Southern
      1. Burungi
      2. Goroa
      3. Alawa
      4. Iragw
      5. Mbugu
      6. Sanye
IV. Chad
  A. West
      1. Hausa
      2. Ngizim
      3. Bolewa Group
        a. Nonplateau Subgroup

          (1) Bolewa
          (2) Dera (Kanakuru)
          (3) Kare
          (4) Mahe
          (5) Ngamo
      b. Plateau Subgroup
          (1) Angas
          (2) Sura

B. East
   1. Bata
      a. Bata Subgroup
          (1) Bachama
          (2) Cheke
          (3) Fali (Jilbw)
          (4) Fali (Mubi)
          (5) Gudu
          (6) Nzangi
          (7) Sukur
          (8) Zumu
      b. Higi Subgroup
          (1) Fali (Kiria)
          (2) Higi
          (3) Vizik
      c. Bura Subgroup
          (1) Bura
          (2) Chibak
          (3) Kilba
          (4) Margi
          (5) West Margi
          (6) Podoko
   2. Tera
      a. Western Subgroup
          (1) Jara
          (2) Pidlindi (Hina)
          (3) Tera
      b. Eastern Subgroup
          (1) Boga
          (2) Gabin

        (3) Hana
- V. Semitic
  - A. Eastern (Akkadian)
    1. Assyrian
    2. Babylonian
  - B. Western
    1. Northwest
       - a. Canaanite
         - (1) Old Canaanite
         - (2) Ugaritic
         - (3) Phoenician
         - (4) Hebrew
         - (5) Moabite
       - b. Aramaic
         - (1) Western
           - (a) Old Aramaic
             - 1) Hama
             - 2) Zinjirli
             - 3) Palmyrene
             - 4) Nabataean
             - 5) Sinaitic
           - (b) Biblical Aramaic (Chaldean)
           - (c) Judaeo-Aramaic (of the Targums and the Palestinian Talmud)
           - (d) Christian Palestinian Aramaic
           - (e) Samaritan
         - (2) Eastern
           - (a) Judaeo-Aramaic (of the Babylonian Talmud)
           - (b) Mandaean
           - (c) Syriac
           - (d) Harranian
    2. Southwest
       - a. North Arabic
       - b. South Arabic
         - (1) Minaean
         - (2) Sabaean
         - (3) Qathabanian

      (4) Hadramautian
      (5) Mahri
      (6) Qarawi
      (7) Sogothri
  c. Ethiopic
      (1) Tigrina (or Tigray)
      (2) Tigre
      (3) Amharic
      (4) Gafat
      (5) Argobba
      (6) Harari
      (7) Gurage

THE NIGER-KORDOFANIAN FAMILY

I. Niger-Congo
  A. West Atlantic
    1. Northern
      a. Wolof
      b. Serer-Sin
      c. Fulani
      d. Serer-Non
      e. Konyagi
      f. Basari
      g. Biafada
      h. Badyara
      i. Dyola
      j. Mandyak
      k. Balante
      l. Banyun
      m. Nalu
      n. Cobiana
      o. Cassanga
      p. Bidyogo
    2. Southern
      a. Temne
      b. Baga

      c. Landoma
      d. Kissi
      e. Bulom
      f. Limba
      g. Gola

B. Mande
    1. Western
      a. Soninke
      b. Malinke
      c. Bambara
      d. Dyula
      e. Numu
      f. Ligbi
      g. Huela
      h. Vai
      i. Kono
      j. Koranko
      k. Khasonke
      l. Susu
      m. Dyalonke
    2. Eastern
      a. Mano Group
        (1) Mano
        (2) Dan (Gio)
        (3) Kweni (Guro)
        (4) Mwa
        (5) Nwa
      b. Samo Group
        (1) Samo
        (2) Bisa
        (3) Busa

C. Gur
    1. Senufo
      a. Minianka
      b. Tagba
      c. Foro
      d. Tegwana (Takponin)
      e. Dyimini

      f. Nafana
2. Lobi-Dogon
      a. Lobi
      b. Dyan
      c. Puguli
      d. Gan
      e. Gouin
      f. Turuka
      g. Doghosie
      h. Doghosie-Fing
      i. Kyan
      j. Tara
      k. Bwamu
      l. Wara
      m. Natioro
      n. Dogon
      o. Kulango
3. Grusi
      a. Awuna
      b. Kasena
      c. Numuna
      d. Lyele
      e. Tomprusi
      f. Kanjaga (Bulea)
      g. Degha
      h. Siti
      i. Kurumba (Fulse)
      j. Sisala
4. Mossi Group
      a. Mossi
      b. Dagomba
      c. Kusasi
      d. Nankanse
      e. Talensi
      f. Mamprusi
      g. Wala
      h. Dagari
      i. Birifo

       j. Namnam
- 5. Tem Group
  - a. Tem
  - b. Kabre
  - c. Delo
  - d. Chala
- 6. Bargu (Bariba)
- 7. Gurma Group
  - a. Gurma
  - b. Tobote (Basari)
  - c. Kasele (Chamba)
  - d. Moba

D. Kwa
- 1. Kru
  - a. Bete
  - b. Bakwe
  - c. Grebo
  - d. Bassa
  - e. De
  - f. Kru (Krawi)
- 2. Avatime Group
  - a. Avatime
  - b. Nyangbo
  - c. Tafi
  - d. Logba
  - e. Likpe
  - f. Ahlo
  - g. Akposo
  - h. Lefana
  - i. Bowili
  - j. Akpafu
  - k. Santrokofi
  - l. Adele
  - m. Kebu
  - n. Anyimere
  - o. Ewe
  - p. Aladian
  - q. Avikam

        r. Gwa
        s. Kyama
        t. Akye
        u. Ari
        v. Abe
        w. Adyukru
        x. Akan
        y. Ga
        z. Adangme
   3. Yoruba Group
        a. Yoruba
        b. Igala
   4. Nupe Group
        a. Nupe
        b. Gbari
        c. Igbira
        d. Gade
   5. Bini Group
        a. Bini
        b. Ishan
        c. Kukuruku
        d. Sobo
   6. Idoma Group
        a. Idoma
        b. Agatu
        c. Iyala
   7. Ibo
   8. Ijo
E. Benue-Congo
   1. Plateau
        a. Kambari-Piti
           (1) Kambari Group
               (a) Kambari
               (b) Dukawa
               (c) Kakakari
               (d) Basa
               (e) Kumuku
               (f) Reshe

    (2) Piti Group
       (a) Piti
       (b) Janji
       (c) Kurana
       (d) Chawai
       (e) Anaguta
       (f) Buj
       (g) Amap
       (h) Gure
       (i) Kahugu
       (j) Ribina
       (k) Butawa
       (l) Kudawa

b. Afusare Group
    (1) Afusare
    (2) Irigwe
    (3) Katab
    (4) Kagoro
    (5) Kaje
    (6) Kachicheri
    (7) Morwa
    (8) Jaba
    (9) Kamantan
    (10) Kadara
    (11) Koro
    (12) Afo

c. Birom Group
    (1) Birom
    (2) Ganawuri (Aten)

d. Rukuba Group
    (1) Rukuba
    (2) Nizam
    (3) Ayu
    (4) Mada
    (5) Kaninkwom

e. Eggon Group
    (1) Eggon
    (2) Nugu

       (3) Yeskwa
- f. Kaleri Group
  - (1) Kaleri
  - (2) Pyem
  - (3) Pai
- g. Yergam-Basherawa
  - (1) Yergam
  - (2) Basherawa

2. Jukunoid
   - a. Jukun
   - b. Kentu
   - c. Nyidu
   - d. Tigong
   - e. Eregba
   - f. Mbembe
   - g. Zumper (Kutev, Mbarike)
   - h. Boritsu

3. Cross-River
   - a. Boki Group
     - (1) Boki
     - (2) Gayi (Uge)
     - (3) Yakorə
   - b. Ibibio Group
     - (1) Ibibio
     - (2) Efik
     - (3) Ogoni (Kana)
     - (4) Andoni
     - (5) Akoiyang
     - (6) Ododop
     - (7) Korop
   - c. Akunakuna Group
     - (1) Akunakuna
     - (2) Abine
     - (3) Yako
     - (4) Asiga
     - (5) Ekuri
     - (6) Ukelle
     - (7) Okpoto-Mteze

4. Bantoid
   a. Tive
   b. Bitare
   c. Batu
   d. Ndoro
   e. Mambila
   f. Bute
   g. Bantu
F. Adamawa-Eastern
   1. Adamawa
      a. Tula Group
         (1) Tula
         (2) Dadiya
         (3) Waja
         (4) Cham
         (5) Kamu
      b. Chamba Group
         (1) Chamba
         (2) Donga
         (3) Lekon
         (4) Wom
         (5) Mumbake
      c. Daka-Taram
         (1) Daka
         (2) Taram
      d. Vere Group
         (1) Vere
         (2) Namshi
         (3) Kolbila
         (4) Pape
         (5) Sari
         (6) Sewe
         (7) Woko
         (8) Kotopo
         (9) Kutin
         (10) Durru
      e. Mumuye Group
         (1) Mumuye

   (2) Kumba
   (3) Gengle
   (4) Teme
   (5) Waka
   (6) Yendang
   (7) Zinna
  f. Dama Group
   (1) Dama
   (2) Mono
   (3) Mbere
   (4) Mundang
   (5) Yasing
   (6) Mangbei
   (7) Mbum
   (8) Kpere
   (9) Lakka
   (10) Dek
  g. Yungur Group
   (1) Yungur
   (2) Mboi
   (3) Libo
   (4) Roba
  h. Kam
  i. Jen-Munga
   (1) Jen
   (2) Munga
  j. Longuda
  k. Fali
  l. Nimbari
  m. Bua Group
   (1) Bua
   (2) Nielim
   (3) Koke
  n. Masa
 2. Eastern
  a. Gbaya Group
   (1) Gbaya
   (2) Manja

      (3) Mbaka
- b. Banda
- c. Ngbandi Group
  - (1) Ngbandi
  - (2) Sango
  - (3) Yakoma
- d. Zarde Group
  - (1) Zarke
  - (2) Nzarkara
  - (3) Barambo
  - (4) Pambia
- e. Bwaka Group
  - (1) Bwaka
  - (2) Monjombo
  - (3) Gbanziri
  - (4) Mundu
  - (5) Mayogo
  - (6) Bangba
- f. Ndogo Group
  - (1) Ndogo
  - (2) Bai
  - (3) Bviri
  - (4) Golo
  - (5) Sere
  - (6) Tagbo
  - (7) Feroge
  - (8) Indri
  - (9) Mangaya
  - (10) Mogoyo
- g. Amadi (Madyo, Ma)
- h. Mondunga-Mba
  - (1) Mondunga
  - (2) Mba (Bamanga)

II. Kordofanian
   A. Koalib
      1. Koalib
      2. Kanderma

  3. Heiban
  4. Laro
  5. Otoro
  6. Kawama
  7. Shwai
  8. Tira
  9. Moro
  10. Fungor
B. Tegali Group
  1. Tegali
  2. Rashad
  3. Tago
  4. Tunale
  5. Moreb
C. Talodi Group
  1. Talodi
  2. Lafofa
  3. Eliri
  4. Masakin
  5. Tacho
  6. Lumun
  7. El Amira
D. Tumtum Group
  1. Tumtum
  2. Tuleshi
  3. Keiga
  4. Korondi
  5. Krongo
  6. Miri
  7. Kadugli
  8. Katcha
E. Katla Group
  1. Katla
  2. Tima

THE NILO-SAHARAN FAMILY

  I. Songhai
 II. Saharan
     A. Kanuri-Kembu
        1. Kanuri
        2. Kembu
     B. Teda-Daza
        1. Teda
        2. Daza
     C. Zaghawa-Berti
        1. Zaghawa
        2. Berti
III. Maban
     A. Maba
     B. Runga
     C. Mimi
     D. Mime
 IV. Fur
  V. Chari-Nile
     A. Nubian
        1. Nile Nubian
           a. Mahas-Fadidja
           b. Kenuzi-Dongola
        2. Kordofanian Nubian
           a. Dair
           b. Dilling
           c. Gulfan
           d. Garko
           e. Kadero
           f. Kundugr
        3. Midob
        4. Birked
     B. Murle Group
        1. Murle
        2. Longarim

    3. Didinga
    4. Suri
    5. Mekan
    6. Murzu
    7. Surma (Including Tirma and Zulmanu)
    8. Masongo
C. Barea
D. Ingassana
E. Nyima-Afitti
    1. Nyima
    2. Afitti
F. Temein-Teis-um-Danab
    1. Temein
    2. Teis-um-Danab
G. Merarit Group
    1. Merarit
    2. Tama
    3. Sungor
H. Dagu Group
    1. Darfur Dagu
    2. Baygo
    3. Sila
    4. Dar Dagu (Wadai)
    5. Western Kordofan Dagu
    6. Njalgulgule
    7. Shatt
    8. Liguri
I. Nilotic
    1. Western
        a. Burum
        b. Shilluk Group
            (1) Shilluk
            (2) Anuak
            (3) Acholi
            (4) Lango
            (5) Alur
            (6) Luo
            (7) Jur

            (8) Bor
        c. Dinka-Nuer
            (1) Dinka
            (2) Nuer
    2. Eastern
        a. Bari Group
            (1) Bari
            (2) Fajulu
            (3) Kakwa
            (4) Mondari
        b. Jie-Masai Group
            (1) Jie Subgroup
                (a) Jie
                (b) Dodoth
                (c) Karamojong
                (d) Teso
                (e) Topotha
                (f) Turkana
            (2) Masai
        c. Southern
            (1) Nandi
            (2) Suk
            (3) Tatoga
    J. Nyangiya-Teuso
        1. Nyangiya
        2. Teuso
VI. Coman
    A. Koma
    B. Ganza
    C. Uduk
    D. Gule
    E. Gumuz
    F. Mao

THE SOUTHEAST ASIATIC FAMILY

I. Munda (Kolarian)
  A. Northern (or Himalayan)
    1. Manchati (Patni)
    2. Kanawri
    3. Bunan
    4. Limbu
    5. Dhimal
  B. Southern (or Chota-Nagpur)
    1. Santali
    2. Mundari
    3. Bhumij
    4. Koda
    5. Asuri
    6. Kurku
II. Mon-Khmer
  A. Central
    1. Mon (or Talaing)
    2. Khmer (or Cambodian)
    3. Bahnar
  B. Eastern
    1. Cham
    2. Sedang
  C. Malaccan
    1. Semang
    2. Sakai
    3. Yakun
  D. Nicobarese
  E. Khasi
  F. Salwen Basin
    1. Palaung
    2. Wa
III. Annam-Muong
  A. Annamese
    1. Upper Annamese

    2. Tongkingese
    3. Cochin-Chinese
  B. Muong
    1. Northern
    2. Central
    3. Southern

Observations: This family contains a great number of additional languages, and different authorities group the members in slightly varying ways. Also, some scholars have suggested distant relationships with other large families (Austronesian; Sino-Tibetan), but the simple fact is that not enough work has yet been done on this group for certainty regarding any of the tentative assertions. The outline given here should be regarded as speculative and incomplete.

THE AUSTRONESIAN FAMILY

I. West
  A. West Indonesian
    1. Sundic
      (a) Javo-Sumatra
        (1) Malayic
          a) Malayan
            1) Malay
            2) Mirangkabau
            3) Kerintji
          b) Madurese
          c) Achinese
          d) Lampurgic
            1) Lampung
            2) Kroë
        (2) Sundanese
        (3) Javanese
      (b) Sasak
      (c) Balinese
      (d) Gayo

       (e) Dayek
           (1) Sampitic
               a) Sampit
               b) Katingan
           (2) Ngadju
    2. Batak
       (a) Toba-Angkola
       (b) Sinalungun
       (c) Karo
    3. Cru
B. Celebes
    1. Bareic
       (a) Baree
       (b) Linduan
    2. Bugic
       (a) Macassarese
       (b) Buginese
C. Gorontalic
    1. Gorontalo
    2. Suwawa
D. Ambic
    1. Ambonese
    2. Paulohi
E. Bigic
    1. Bulic
       (a) Buli
       (b) Minyafruin
    2. As
    3. Biga
F. Sarmic
    1. Sobeic
       (a) Sobei
       (b) Moar
    2. Tarpic
       (a) Tarpia
       (b) Bonggo
G. Geelvink
    1. Biakic

          (a) Biak
          (b) Numfor
     2. Wandamic
          (a) Wandamen
          (b) Japen
  H. Hollandia
     1. Tobatic
          (a) Tobati
          (b) Kajupulaw
     2. Ormu
II. Northwest
  A. Atayalic
     1. Atayal
     2. Seedik
  B. East Formosan
     1. Ami
     2. Paiwan
     3. Bunun
     4. Thao
  C. Philippine
     1. Sulic
          (a) Mesophilippine
             (1) Tagalic
               a) Bisayan
                  1) Cebuan
                  2) Butu
                  3) Ilonggo
                  4) Cuyunon
               b) Cagayanon
               c) Manmanua
               d) Tagalog
             (2) Bikol
             (3) Mansakic
               a) Mansaka
               b) Tagakaolo
             (4) Hanunoic
               a) Hanunoo
               b) Buhid

                (5) Irayic
                    a) Alangic
                        1) Iraya
                        2) Alangan
                    b) Nauhan
                (6) Subanun
            (b) Dibabaic
                (1) Dibabaon
                (2) Agusan-Manobo
            (c) Kalamian
            (d) Palawanic
            (d) Palawanic
                (1) Palawano
                (2) Babuyan
                (3) Tagbanua
            (e) Bukidnic
                (1) Bukidnon
                (2) Central Manobo
            (f) Pampangan
            (g) Cotabato-Manobo
    2. Maranao
    3. Casiguran
    4. Yakan
    5. Baler
    6. Tiruray
    7. Murutic
        (a) Murut
        (b) Tarakan
        (c) Bolongan
    8. Dusan
    9. Bilic
        (a) Bilaan
        (b) Tagabili
    10. Ivatan
    11. Cordilleran
        (a) Inibaloy
        (b) North Cordilleran
            (1) Banagic

      a) Isneg
         1) Itawic
            a— Itawi
            b— Malaweg
         2) Barran
         3) Bayag
      b) Ibanag
      c) Gaddang
         1) Christian Gaddang
         2) Pagan Gaddang
      d) Atok
      e) Yogad
    (2) Ilocano
    (3) Kalinga
      a) Balbalasang
      b) Pinukpuk
    (4) Igorot
      a) Kankanay
      b) Sagada
      c) Bontok
      d) Bayyu
    (5) Ifugao
      a) Kiangan
      b) Mayaoyao
      c) Hanglulic
         1) Hanglulu
         2) Kanguya
    (6) Piggattan
    (7) Isinay
III. North and East
  A. Carolinian
    1. Ponapean
    2. Trukic
      (a) Trukese
      (b) Wolean
    3. Marshallese
    4. Kusaiean

B. Polynesian
    1. West Polynesian
        (a) Tongic
            (1) Tongan
            (2) Niue
        (b) Ellicean
            (1) Ellice
            (2) Tikopia
        (c) Rennell
        (d) Samoan
        (e) Pileni
    2. East Polynesian
        (a) Rarotongan
        (b) Hawaii
        (c) Easter
        (d) Marquesas
        (e) Tahitian
    3. Maori
    4. Kapingamarangi
    5. Nukuoro

IV. Central
  A. Massim
    1. Wedauic
        (a) Wedauan
        (b) Keheraran
    2. Dobic
        (a) Dobu
        (b) Molima
  B. Uvolic
    1. Uvol
    2. Mamusic
        (a) Mamusi
        (b) Mengen
  C. Buka
    1. Northwest Bukas
        (a) Petatsic
            (1) Petats

          (2) Sumoun
      (b) Halian
          (1) Hanahan
          (2) Lontes
   2. Teopic
      (a) Teop
      (b) Raosiara
      (c) Saposa
D. Choiseul
   1. Ririan
      (a) Sengan
      (b) Ririo
   2. Varisian
      (a) Varisi
      (b) Vagua
E. New Georgian
   1. Rovianic
      (a) Roviana
      (b) Kusagean
   2. Marovan
   3. Lunggic
      (a) Lunggan
      (b) Duke
F. Lauic
   1. Lau
   2. Toqabaita
G. Loyalty
   1. Dehu
   2. Nengone
   3. Iai
H. North New Caledonian
   1. Camuhic
      (a) Haekic
          (1) Haeke
          (2) Pwamei
      (b) Camuhi
   2. Thuangic
      (a) Thuanga

      (b) Fwagumwak
    3. Paici
I.   South New Caledonian
    1. Wailic
      (a) Houailou
      (b) Haragure
    2. Hameha
    3. Numeic
      (a) Nadubea
      (b) Kwenyi

THE SINO-TIBETAN FAMILY

I. Tibeto-Burman
   A. Tibeto-Himalayan
      1. Tibetan
      2. Himalayan
         a. Sunvar
         b. Gurung
         c. Lepcha (or Rong)
         d. Toto
   B. North Assamese
      1. Aka
      2. Dafla
      3. Abor-Miri
      4. Mishmi
   C. Middle and South Assamese
      1. Bodo
      2. Naga-Bodo
      3. Naga
      4. Lhota
      5. Tableng
      6. Kachin (or Sing-pho)
      7. Naga-Kuki
   D. Arakan-Burmese
      1. Kuki-Chin
         a. Meithei

        b. Thado
        c. Shunkla (or Tashon)
        d. Lai
        e. Purum
        f. Lushei
     2. Old Kuki
        a. Rankhol
        b. Sho
        c. Khyang
        d. Khami
     3. Burmese
        a. Maghi (or Burmese proper)
        b. Arakanese
        c. Mru
II. Tai-Chinese
  A. Chinese
     1. Mandarin
        a. Northern (the basis for the Kuo-Yu)
        b. Southern
        c. Southwestern
     2. Cantonese
     3. Kan-Hakka
     4. Min Group
        a. Foochow
        b. Amoy-Swatow
     5. Wu
        a. Shanghai
        b. Wenchow
     6. Hsiang (Hunan)
  B. Si-lo-mo
  C. Karen
     1. Sgaw
     2. Pwo
     3. Taungthu
     4. Bghai
  D. Tai
     1. Southeastern
        a. Siamese
        b. Laotian

    c. Lü
    d. Knün
  2. Eastern
    a. Li
    b. Dioi
  3. Northern
    a. Miao
    b. Yao
    c. Khamti
    d. Ahom (extinct)

OBSERVATIONS

This listing is both incomplete and, as seen in the great dis-
agreements among the very few scholars who have seriously dealt
with the entire family, highly uncertain. Robert Shafer's *Bibliography of the Sino-Tibetan Languages* (Wiesbaden, 1957) provides
a useful guide to the available literature pertaining to the subject.
Individual (but, unfortunately, limited) studies of specific subgroups
of the family have been appearing in recent years, and, ultimately
a reliable overview and reclassification of the total genetic group
should emerge. One such reanalysis is Robbins Burling's *Proto-Lolo-
Burmese* (Indiana University Research Center in Anthropology,
Folklore, and Linguistics, Publication 43, 1967). Burling deals with
six languages of the Tibeto-Burman subgroup which he groups
together as follows:

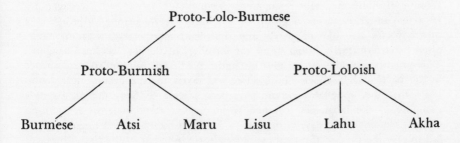

Fig. 11

What is of major consequence is Burling's presentation of the basis for the classification, with supporting evidence.

NOTES

As a general reference work on the classification of languages, *Les Langues du Monde,* prepared by a group of linguists under the direction of A. Meillet and Marcel Cohen (Paris: Centre National de la Recherche Scientifique, 1952), is highly useful. However no one work can possibly give a complete picture of the full and complex range of interrelationships. The more recent appearance of various grammars, dictionaries, and shorter studies has provided additional tools for more accurate analyses and consequent improvements in some of the classificational schemes. Languages formerly either grouped together or not on the basis of inadequate, sometimes nonlinguistic, evidence are now being subjected to sound linguistic analysis with, in at least some instances, a consequent reclassification. For example, in 1967 Samuel Martin demonstrated that Japanese and Korean were definitely related to each other, a fact suspected but not actually proven for over a century. Following this observation, Roy Andrew Miller listed the Japanese-Korean group as a subdivision of Altaic. In like fashion, the Chad languages of Central Africa were shown to be part of the Afro-Asiatic (Hamito-Semitic) family. Then the Chad family itself was recognized as much wider in extent than previously believed. Through these and other observations of the same sort a picture has been emerging of larger and larger groupings of genetically related super families. The outlines of the families listed in this section are intended to be helpful, but, at least for some of the groups not yet fully or adequately studied, no claim can be or is made regarding completeness or accuracy. Certainly a good deal more is known about those language families, such as Indo-European, which have been the subject of long and extensive investigation by countless scholars. Where recent studies suggest changes in the traditional views, the results of these analyses have been incorporated, without comment, into the groupings.

For the most part, the outlines of the African languages follow Joseph Greenberg's classifications, but with some minor modifications designed to take account of additional, albeit sometimes fragmentary, specialized investigations. In a few instances where a group of languages clearly belongs together as a subgroup, for the sake of clarity and time-depth perspective, a group name, often taken arbitrarily from one of the members of the set, has been assigned. This practice would seem to give an undeserved and unintended prominence to the particular language whose name was taken for the group, and, doubtless, some other appellation would have been preferable. Nevertheless, a simple grouping of the languages together, without some terminological recognition of joint, common ancestry, as opposed to more distantly related tongues might fail to give the proper historical overview clearly inherent in the linguistic facts.

The classification of the Austronesian group has generally followed Isidore Dyen's *A Lexicostatistical Classification of the Austronesian Languages* (Indiana University Publications in Anthropology and Linguistics, Monograph No. 19, 1965), but with the deletion of the names of some languages whose position in the family is uncertain or controversial. The current work, aimed predominantly at providing methodological perspective, did not seem to be an appropriate forum for the lengthy and somewhat highly specialized discussion or analysis that would be necessary to the settling of such problems.